We were made to image God as beautiful community. We most brilliantly reflect God's glory to the world when we are united in love under the lordship of Jesus Christ across lines of difference. A persistent question is, "how do we get there?" Maria Garriott has done us a wonderful service in *Stronger Together*. Maria is a friend from whom I've learned a great deal over the years, and she has taught me well again. This book is full of theological depth and practical wisdom. Maria is right, "The Kingdom of God feels reckless. Following Jesus isn't a call to comfort: it is a call to growth and to change." Take this journey with her and be equipped to grow and change into a more magnificent reflection of our beautiful God.

—Rev. Irwyn L. Ince, D.Min.
Author, *The Beautiful Community*
Founder, Institute for Cross Cultural Mission
MNA Coordinator Pro Tempore

Stronger Together is a courageous book that the Church needs. In an ecclesiastical environment often sharply divided by politics and presumption, to the extent that we don't want to 'go there,' Garriott enters in. She is unafraid to speak into the pain that besets our society and culture – with Jesus and his good news. And she graciously appeals to the Church to consider past sins. Her only loyalty is the gospel, and this lends to balanced reason. Through personal reflections and careful study, she pares much of the confusing landscape of terms and misconceptions that so easily divide into digestible biblical insights that enable peaceful contemplation and dialogue. I gladly endorse this book.

—Mike Khandjian
Pastor, Chapelgate Presbyterian Church, Maryland
Author of *A Sometimes Stumbling Life*

In *Stronger Together,* Maria invites us to look at racism through the lens of the gospel. Sharing glimpses from her story, America's story, and the church's story, Maria increases our thirst for God's Story where pain is not minimized and hope of renewal is our promised future and present pursuit. Tremble not. Dive in. Read, reflect on God's word, and dialogue with others growing ever STRONGER in love and unity TOGETHER!

—Tami Resch
Co-founder, Parakaleo; Co-founder, AlongsideU
Co-Author, *Beyond Duct Tape: Holding the Heart Together in a Life of Ministry*

I wasn't prepared for the journey that *Stronger Together: A Gospel Lens on Unity*, took me on. Maria's journey of living in an African-American neighborhood, growing a multi-ethnic church and learning her own cultural biases reveal the heart of the Gospel. If you've been confused or heartbroken over the racial tension in our country, if you have felt ill-equipped to engage in conversation around these deep divides, and if you want to better understand God's perspective and how the Gospel is our hope, Maria's book is your new go-to. She expertly weaves her story, biblical narratives and insights and a comprehensive study of our nation's history together, to help us understand how we got here and how we can be a part of the healing. Maria is a humble, experienced voice in the world inviting us to enter into what Jesus has called us to-- real unity. It's His idea.

—Minister Tracey Tiernan Coiro
Bridgeway Community Church
Radio host, 95.1 SHINE-FM, podcast Your Day Brighter

Stronger Together: A Gospel Lens on Unity is well suited for our times. Garriott's book will be an effective tool in helping churches understand reality from the perspective of people with whom they may not agree or understand. This book lends itself to small group discussion and interaction that will help Christians better understand many of our cultural and racial divisions.

—Wy Plummer
African American Ministries Coordinator
Mission to North America (PCA)

I have deep respect for Craig and Maria Garriott, who have spent many years in urban and cross-cultural ministry. Maria is a wonderful writer who is able to recount many of the real life stories she has experienced. Maria creates a quilt reflecting on issues, national history, personal and church history to move us toward greater understanding, and I think greater hope, about what is going on in our country in regard to justice, race, and the response of the church.

—Randy Nabors
Founder, New City Network
Urban and Mercy Ministries Coordinator, PCA
Author, *Merciful: The Opportunity and Challenge of Discipling the Poor out of Poverty* and *Insufficient*

Stronger Together is a timely read for any reader or church that wants to learn from someone who has been a student of the grace found in diverse settings. Maria's book is descriptive more than prescriptive, causing us to long for our churches to courageously walk the line of the gospel, pointing to Christ. *Stronger Together* doesn't just serve as a needed discussion guide, but a celebration of the radical blessing of community within the beautiful Bride of Christ. Maria carefully stirs our hearts for the Day when we will display this community in perfect harmony, penning an invitation for readers to walk in faith towards their spot at the table now, that we may be challenged, encouraged and changed as we experience what only God can do through Christ and in the power of His Spirit!

—Meaghan May
Liaison to Elder's Wives in the PCA

Maria has woven together three storylines in an engaging way: 1) Her own experience planting a multi-cultural inner-city church with her husband Craig when they were young and naive about race and culture. 2) The sad legacy of slavery and ongoing racism in our country. 3) God's heart to create for His glory a single family of His children, united in Christ from every nation, tribe, people and language (Rev 7:9). I especially appreciate Maria's transparency about her own journey, and openness to the Holy Spirit's work in her heart. I encourage you to read with the same openness.

—Chris Sicks
Pastor of One Voice Fellowship
Author of *Tangible: Making God Known through Deeds of Mercy and Words of Truth.*

If you long for your church to reflect that deep and practical unity in diversity to which Christ clearly calls us, accessing the power his death and resurrection makes available to us, Maria Garriott's *Stronger Together* is a valuable and compelling tool. Each chapter begins with an engaging episode from the Garriotts' decades of grappling with the challenges of unity in Christ as they planted an intentionally multicultural church in an urban neighborhood where they were the minority, followed by an exploration of the Biblical truths and hard-won insights that have illuminated their journey. A U.S. History Window in each chapter brings into focus some unseen roots of the issues that we have allowed to disrupt and destroy the unity of our churches – and our witness to unbelievers – today. And the Bible study for each chapter invites readers to process what they have read, alone or in groups, in the light of Scripture, providing an abundance of resources, both print and online. "Unity is messy," Garriott says, but, for believers eager to demonstrate Christ's reconciling power in a hurting world, "it is not optional."

—Pat Hatch
Refugee and Immigrant Ministry Director
PCA Mission to North America

This book is a wonderful mixture of approachability and warmth via the author's personal stories, straight talk about the complexities of intercultural relationships in our country's past and present, and our roles as individuals to bring about a more Christlike orientation to our relationships as well as addressing societal inequities. It is steeped in thoroughly biblical wisdom to address the questions we all have about needful growth in this area. The study questions for each chapter are thought provoking and well designed for personal or group use. It is a beneficial resource to anyone looking to grow in intercultural awareness and competence.

—Ann Powers
Midwest Alliance Church Planting Partnership
Christian Cultural Intelligence Group

Maria's book is a call to open our eyes and hearts to hear the pains of the weary and the disenchanted... She entices the reader to consider what the Lord may be asking us to do in a world marred by brokenness and increasingly filled with vain philosophies. Maria gently takes our hand as she leads on a pilgrimage of historical reflections on the ways the gospel confronts class, ethnic and structural inequalities. It is a soulful journey. This book is an offering for those daring enough to read it. By the power of the gospel, we are "Stronger Together."

—Dr. Louis H. Wilson
Pastor, New Song Community Church

Maria Garriott's deeply personal, honest and vulnerable writing compels readers to reflect on their own journeys, successes, and failures toward unity. *Stronger Together* encourages us to continue to lean in, despite the many ongoing challenges of reconciliation. I have learned much from Maria, for which I am grateful to the Lord. This book serves as an important reminder to embrace our collective call toward Christ-centered unity.
—Alexander Jun, Ph.D.
Author, *White Jesus* and *White Evolution*
Professor of Higher Education, Azusa Pacific University

STRONGER TOGETHER

A Gospel Lens on Unity

MARIA GARRIOTT

Stronger Together
Copyright © 2021 Maria Garriott

All rights reserved. This book is protected by copyright laws of the United States of America. This book may not be copied or reprinted for commercial gain or profit.

Unless otherwise indicated, Scripture quotations are from The Holy Bible, English Standard Version © (ESV©), copyright 2001 by Crossway. Used by permission. All rights reserved.

Scripture quotations marked (NIV) are taken from the Holy Bible, New International Version®, NIV®. Copyright © 1973, 1978, 1984, 2011 by Biblica, Inc.™ Used by permission of Zondervan. All rights reserved worldwide. www.zondervan.com. The "NIV" and "New International Version" are trademarks registered in the United States Patent and Trademark Office by Biblica, Inc.

An earlier version of "A Uniting Savior, Diverse Friendships" appeared in *Beyond the Roles*, ed. by Melanie Cogdill (CDM, 2019).

An earlier version of "Race, Redemption and the Multiethnic Church" appeared in *Breakpoint Magazine* (Jan/Feb. 2007).

Cover photo: Julian Hague
Author photo: Craig Garriott
Interior and cover design: Jenny Erlingsson, Milk & Honey Books, LLC

Print ISBN 13: 978-0-9974631-7-0

For Worldwide Distribution

"My prayer is not for them alone. I pray also for those who will believe in me through their message, that all of them may be one, Father, just as you are in me, and I am in you. May they also be in us so that the world may believe that you have sent me. I have given them the glory that you gave me, that they may be one as we are one—I in them and you in me—so that they may be brought to complete unity. Then the world will know that you sent me and have loved them even as you have loved me."

John 17:20-23 (NIV)

An Invitation

Welcome to beauty and brokenness. To humility and repentance. To joy and deeper relationships. Be prepared for a beautiful struggle. You may feel unsettled, confused, or excited. Or all three.

My prayer is that in *Stronger Together*, you will see Jesus more clearly. That as you understand more of the heart of God and the beauty of his diverse peoples, you will see his reflection in brothers and sisters from different ethnicities, cultures, races, backgrounds, and abilities. That you will fall in love afresh with Jesus, and experience his heart for those the world separates, overlooks, or even disdains. That you will joyfully anticipate that marriage feast of the Lamb when believers from every tribe, people, and tongue bring our unique languages, personalities, life stories, and ethnicities before his throne, united in worship. That as you know more of the fullness of God's people, you will know more of the fullness of God.

In Jesus's final prayer before his crucifixion in John 17, he prayed that his followers "may all be one, just as you,

Father, are in me, and I in you, that they also may be in us." The Greek for "just as" in this passage is sometimes used in mathematical formulas: equal amounts, equivalent to, the same as.

How can that be? The Father, Son, and Spirit are united, and Jesus dies to bring us into that relationship. Our unity is so supernatural that when we get it right, onlookers marvel. Our unity testifies to who Jesus is. May we, even as sinners in the midst of our fractious world, be one in him.

How To Use This Book

The seeds of this book began to sprout forty years ago, when my husband Craig and I moved into Baltimore City as newlyweds to start a multiethnic church. Baltimore was a historically Black-White city scarred by segregation, White flight, racial riots, and the loss of industrial jobs. The crack epidemic, mass incarceration, and other ills would compound this misery. In the ensuing decades, newer immigrants flocked to Baltimore, creating an even richer diversity.

The Bible taught that the gospel of Jesus Christ united rich and poor, enslaved and free, and Jew and Gentile into one family. Historical animosities were healed. Wealthier believers helped those who had fallen on hard times. Could this happen in Baltimore? Could Jesus still unite historically divided groups today? We believed the Bible provided the foundation and unique spiritual tools and power for racial and ethnic unity.

We started chipping away at our ignorance, reading books, listening to neighbors, and learning from older urban ministry practitioners. The cultural history of the

New Testament helped us apply Scripture to present-day problems. For example, why did the distribution of food to Hebraic and Greek widows in Acts 6 go wrong? How did the leaders correct this? After Jesus's first recorded sermon, why did his hearers shift from "all spoke well of him" to being "filled with wrath" (Luke 4)? How can knowing the cultural background of these passages deepen our understanding and guide us today?

American history, church history, and sociology helped us too. To understand our present, we must know our history. As the Southern novelist William Faulkner wrote, "The past is never dead. It's not even past." History—both what has been taught and what has been neglected or erased from the historical record—explains how we arrived at this cultural moment. From sociology—the study of social institutions and structures—we learn how our laws, institutions, and history affect us today.

This book flows from a passion to see God's reconciled community on earth "as it is in heaven." Each chapter begins with a story of how my husband and I grappled with the challenges of unity. An explanation of biblical truths related to the topic follows. A bite-sized "History Window" is included in each chapter to provide greater context on America's racial and ethnic past.

Finally, a Bible study for each chapter is included for individual or group study.

The website www.strongertogethergospel.com provides additional resources.

Discussing the book and Bible study as part of a group will help cement your learning and provide deep fellowship. Your discussion will be especially stimulating if your group includes people from different backgrounds, life stages, ethnicities, or races.

I hope this book will encourage the church and build unity among God's people. The Apostle James says we are to be doers of the word, not just hearers. We don't want big heads and small hearts; knowledge must be fused with practice. May you be blessed by hearing, reading, and doing.

TABLE OF CONTENTS

THE GOSPEL, UNITY, AND YOU 17

HOW THE GOSPEL FREES US 27

THE GOSPEL UNITES US 35

JESUS, THE BARRIER BREAKER 43

CULTURE AND GOD'S STORY OF GRACE 51

CULTURE, CREATION, AND FALL 57

CULTURE, REDEMPTION, AND RESTORATION 65

THE EARLY CHURCH MEETS CULTURE 73

HOW DIVERSITY BENEFITS THE CHURCH 81

RACE, REDEMPTION, AND THE MULTIETHNIC CHURCH 91

THE MISEDUCATION OF MARIA GARRIOTT 101

SOCIAL JUSTICE? BIBLICAL JUSTICE? 109

REPENTING AND LAMENTING 119

PRIVILEGES AND RIGHTS 129

REPAIRING WHAT IS BROKEN 141

HOSPITALITY 149

A HARDER BRIDGE TO CROSS	161
PARTNERING WITH GOD IN RESTORATION	169
BIBLE STUDY & DISCUSSION GUIDE	181
ACKNOWLEDGEMENTS	242
ABOUT THE AUTHOR	244
BIBLIOGRAPHY	246
ENDNOTES	262

Chapter 1

The Gospel, Unity, and You

Entering In: My Cross-Cultural Story

In 1980, shortly after our wedding, our denomination asked my husband Craig to lead a fledgling church in Baltimore. The previous pastor had been dismissed. They asked even though Craig was just an intern pastor at a suburban church and hadn't finished his three-year seminary degree, and we had no prior urban experience. If a handful of believers in a city neighborhood wanted to start a church, perhaps we could help. I was 21. Craig was 26. We lacked wisdom, but oozed optimism.

That church transformed our lives.

The group met in the basement of an aging Baptist church. The neighborhood was transitioning from largely White to Black and included an eclectic mix of blue-collar workers, aging hippies, Johns Hopkins students, and older residents. As we arrived for our first service, a man in dirty jeans and denim jacket stood outside the church smoking. He brightened at seeing us and stuck out a nicotine-stained hand. "How ya' doing? I'm Larry." Hard living made him look older than forty. If he hadn't struggled with paranoid schizophrenia, the quick-witted, gregarious Larry would have been a highly successful businessman. Inside, we met the rest of the congregation: two recent Johns Hopkins University graduates, a young married couple, a grad student, and two of Larry's friends who, like him, navigated significant mental illness.

We gathered metal folding chairs in a circle, sang a few songs, prayed, and Craig taught from the Bible. After every service, we shared a potluck dinner; once, Larry brought a six-pack of beer, which did not go over well when the Baptists found his empties. To make sure no one left hungry, I learned to cook generous quantities of inexpensive, filling food: lasagna, spaghetti, chicken casseroles.

In the 1980s, Baltimore's urban ills pressed hard. Restrictive city housing covenants, redlining practices, and White flight had cemented Baltimore's status as a hyper-segregated city. The loss of well-paying jobs at Bethlehem Steel and other industries cut off a once-solid path to the middle class. With a shrinking tax base, city services diminished. Schools struggled. The crack cocaine epidemic, mass incarceration, and the rise of drug gangs deepened racial and economic divides.

What better opportunity to show that Jesus could change lives and bring together people from different classes, races, and backgrounds? The accountant and the 7-Eleven clerk, the doctor and the minimum-wage worker? The upwardly mobile college student and the guy living on disability checks? We dreamed of a multiethnic church reaching all the city, reflecting God's shalom, what Dr. Martin Luther King Jr. had called "the beloved community."

Craig soon realized that this church needed a spiritually strong, city-savvy co-leader. The Lone Ranger-White savior model wasn't biblical or effective; we needed diverse leadership to reach a diverse city. He called Bill Bolling, a friend from college. The oldest of five children raised by a rich-in-faith mother after alcoholism had claimed her husband, Bill knew the streets and survival strategies of the city. He also knew his Bible. Craig persuaded Bill to visit our tiny church. Bill's first thought: "This is a weird group. It will never work."

And yet it did, by God's grace. Bill became an elder at Faith Christian Fellowship, where he still worships and serves today. After struggling for a decade to break the 100-attendee barrier, the church eventually enfolded 400 people. Church members tutored and mentored neighborhood kids, volunteered in church sports leagues, and opened a food pantry. Because many kids in our Sunday School or after-school program couldn't read fluently, we started a Christian elementary school that turned no one away for lack of funds. College and graduate students worshipped with us and then took jobs elsewhere, touching people around the world. Together, we put our faith into practice, obeying the words of the prophet Micah:

> He has told you, O man, what is good; and what does the LORD require of you but to do justice, and to love kindness, and to walk humbly with your God? (Mic. 6:8 NIV)

Creating community with people from different backgrounds, races, ethnicities, and cultures was hard and beautiful. While every community can bruise us, cross-cultural community adds an additional layer of challenge and vulnerability. What if I do something racially insensitive? Or my politics alienate a brother or sister in the faith? Or I expect that my cultural preferences—style of music, length of the service, type of preaching—are "normal" and should be honored? What if church becomes a place of wounding, not healing?

Being in a cross-cultural spiritual community and raising our five children in the church's struggling working-class, largely African American neighborhood forced me to step outside my culture. As I listened to the stories and experiences of other men and women, I began to see the world through different eyes. On Sunday, our worship blended musical styles from multiple cultures: Black gospel, contemporary and historic hymns, jazz, classical music. Occasionally, a bluegrass tune.

God designed community not just for our comfort and edification, but for our spiritual growth. Cross-cultural churches tend to grow more slowly. But they grow deeper. As we live, serve, play, and worship together, we come face-to-face with the approval we long for, the little grievances we want to nurture, the preferences we want to make principles. We mature as we listen to one another, forgive one another, and are honest with ourselves and each other.

> **Unity is messy, but not optional.**

To persevere in cross-cultural community, we must understand God's vision for unity expressed throughout the Bible and stay grounded in our identity in Christ. Unity is messy, but it is not optional and demonstrates Christ's reconciling power. Our identity flows from our adoption as children of God and fuels our perseverance. Any good deeds flow from grace and gratitude, not a desire to earn favor with God or others. Only with this foundational theology and identity can we emerge from the fire of trials wiser and kinder, not bitter and brittle.

> Our adoption as sons and daughters of God is our primary identity, superseding all other identities.

The issues we faced in the 1980s—political and racial division, cultural and demographic shifts, economic disparity, and questions of racial justice—have become front and center. For almost forty years, we hammered out a theology and practice. We made many, many mistakes.

In 2018, we left that pastorate to start Baltimore Antioch Leadership Movement (BALM) to help build the next generation of cross-cultural leaders for the church.

The Kingdom of God feels reckless. Following Jesus isn't a call to comfort: it is a call to growth and to change. We must be willing to give ourselves away, take risks, no matter what our age or season or cost. Let's enter into this life-changing Kingdom adventure of cross-cultural community.

A Deeper Dive: Unity Through a Gospel Lens

In the past, Caucasians in the U.S. have had the luxury of not having to understand and interact sensitively with other cultures to survive, while people in non-dominant cultures (African Americans, Native Americans, Latinos, Asian Americans, and others) have had to be culturally bilingual.

A cursory review of U.S. history shows that those of the dominant culture oppressed, persecuted, and marginalized African Americans and Native Americans. It also reveals shameful episodes against Asian Americans, Latinx Americans, and others (including Irish, Italian, and German immigrants). But racial sin in America is not confined to Caucasians; some non-dominant ethnic groups have also historically been alienated from one another.

Yet the Bible calls us to a higher standard. The gospel of Jesus Christ reconciles us to God, but also reconciles us to one another. Jesus calls us to make disciples of all nations (ethnos), not just those with whom we feel comfortable.

On the eve of his crucifixion, like a high priest in the Old Testament, Jesus interceded to the Father on behalf of the people. He compared our unity as believers to his unity with his Father and the Spirit.

> I do not ask for these only, but also for those who will believe in me through their word, that they may all be one, just as you, Father, are in me, and I in you, that they also may be in us, so that the world may believe that you have sent me. The glory that you have given me I have given to them, that they may be one even as we are one, I in them and you in me, that they may become perfectly one, so that the world may know that you sent me and loved them even as you loved me. (John 17:20-23)

The bedrock principle of Stronger Together is the reality of our unity in Christ. When Jesus died on the cross for our sins and gave us his righteousness, we became part of God's universal, diverse community. Our adoption as sons and daughters of God through Christ is our primary identity, superseding all other categories or identities. Jesus unites us across all racial, cultural, gender, ethnic, and class distinctions. This unity testifies to his supernatural power and is a foretaste of heaven as together we reflect the diversity of God's creation and anticipate his coming kingdom.

Theologian Christine Pohl writes, "The best testimony to the truth of the gospel is the quality of our life together. Jesus risked his reputation and the credibility of his story by tying them to how his followers live and care for one another in community."[1]

While Jesus was able to engage with people from different cultures and was without sin in all things, we are not. The early church was marked by cultural diversity and faced challenges as it grew in grasping the ramifications of this radical unity in Christ. We can too.

Cultural intelligence, or the ability to relate and work effectively across cultures, helps us recognize our own cultural blinders. Our culture—values, behaviors, and ways of thinking—is so deeply rooted in us that we often fail to see it. But if we examine what seems "normal" to us, we can better evaluate these beliefs under the lens of Scripture.

We have much to learn from those who are different from us. These relationships help us develop a more biblical worldview, not an individualized one, and can challenge us to live according to Kingdom values, not cultural preferences.

Stronger Together

As we reflect on Scripture and hear one another's stories, the Holy Spirit changes us. Our goal is to develop a deeper love and appreciation for our brothers and sisters, become more like Jesus, and grow in our ability to proclaim and live out the gospel.

HISTORY WINDOW 1

America, The Church, and Race

In *Narrative of the Life of an American Slave* (1845), Frederick Douglass differentiated between the religion of slaveholding America and true Christianity. "I love the pure, peaceable, and impartial Christianity of Christ: I therefore hate the corrupt, slaveholding, women-whipping, cradle-plundering, partial, and hypocritical Christianity of this land."

Many of the seemingly intractable problems we face today have deep roots. As a nation, we have much to be proud of, yet also much to grieve. America has had opportunities to create a more just nation for *all* its people. Sometimes, we have done so: banning the transatlantic slave trade, ending child labor, enfranchising women, passing civil rights and disabilities legislation. Yet we've often failed to "let justice roll on" (Amos 5:24), both as a nation and as God's people.

From our nation's earliest days, laws were passed that devalued people of color. Native residents were denigrated, displaced, and even destroyed. Slavery fueled the economy for more than 200 years and was followed by other injustices. Asian Americans and Latinos faced significant discrimination. Sadly, the church often cooperated with race prejudice or even promoted it. A fuller understanding of our history, including the church's failures, can help us move toward racial and ethnic reconciliation.

When the Book of the Law was rediscovered during Temple renovations and read to King Josiah (2 Kings 22), he recognized his nation's sin. He lamented that "our fathers have not obeyed the words of this book." He renewed the nation's covenant to obey God's law.

We too must learn from our past, lament, repair, and move toward healing. As one writer notes, "Remembering our nation's virtues helps give us hope. Remembering our sin gives us humility. Remembering both gives us the motivation *and* the inspiration necessary to repair our land."[1]

Chapter 2

How The Gospel Frees Us

How the Gospel Frees Me in Racial Reconciliation

It was a stupid remark from my nervous, 22-year-old self, tossed into our small church's Thanksgiving testimony time without forethought. Referring to the challenges European colonists faced in the New World, I'd used the phrase "savage Indians."

This didn't sit well with Timothy, who was proud of his partial Lumbee tribal heritage. He phoned me to set the record straight. Even worse, I knew better. My father, an avid reader of history, more than once had lamented, "We broke every treaty we made with Native Americans." Although I'd read about Chief Joseph, Sitting Bull, and the Wounded Knee massacre, the stereotypes I'd absorbed through the "Lone Ranger" and other Hollywood films surfaced in that moment.

After I hung up with Timothy, I battled tears of frustration. *That was a stupid thing to say.* And self-justification. *I work so hard every Sunday to help take care of his rambunctious small children.* Even after apologizing, I felt bad about insulting Timothy's heritage.

The problem wasn't Timothy's gentle, private rebuke, but me. I needed a whole lot more gospel. I needed to apply the good news that Jesus accepts me because of who he is. He paid for my sins, so I don't have to justify myself. I shouldn't be surprised or crushed with remorse when I say or do something thoughtless or ugly, but should remember the grace—unmerited favor—of the gospel. "There is therefore no condemnation for those who are in Christ Jesus. For the law of the spirit of life has set you free in Christ Jesus from the law of sin and death" (Rom. 8:1). Because Jesus forgives me, I need to forgive myself. "If we confess our sins, he is faithful and just to forgive our sins, and cleanse us from all unrighteousness"(1 John 1:9). I should repent, apologize, and move on. Embrace the grace.

Depending on others to validate my worth courts disaster. If I make other people's approval something I must have—an idol—I'll respond with anger, depression, or self-justification when my idol is toppled. Approval-seeking is a human problem and an occupational hazard in ministry, where every congregant has different expectations. But if I can face my desire for approval and apply the gospel to it, God will mature me. Criticism will not devastate or trigger self-defense. God will expose my worthless paradigms, and give me joy from a deeper place.

More recently, my careless question unsettled another brother in the faith.

Raji, who had come to the U.S. as a graduate student, had often been to our home. I'd asked innocently, "Now that you've finished your doctorate, will you go back to your home country?"

But my intention—"Will we enjoy your presence here in the future?"— wasn't what he heard. Raji heard echoes of other comments and criticisms he'd absorbed, even from Christians. He heard, "When will you go back to where you came from and stop taking American jobs? We don't want you here."

When he shared this with me, it saddened me that people had been so unwelcoming. While I knew anti-immigrant sentiment existed, it wasn't part of my experience. I apologized and thanked him for telling me. I told him I'd express myself more carefully in the future. I asked him to let me know if I said anything else that offended him. I did not brood, but accepted forgiveness and learned from it. Our relationship was strengthened.

Timothy and Raji are still members of our church today. Both men modeled biblical conflict resolution (Matt. 18:15) by bringing my insensitive comments to my attention directly, and the result was greater unity. We're all growing deeper in our understanding of God and our appreciation of each other.

Our blind spots can be amplified when we cross cultural boundaries. We will make mistakes. We might feel shame or tempted to give up. Yet if we keep re-centering our identity in our status as beloved, forgiven children of God, we are free to fail. And free to apologize, get back up, and try again, secure in the one who embraces his children unconditionally.

A Deeper Dive: Grounded in the Gospel

As we explore our unity in Christ and its applications to all aspects of our life, we must drink again from the well of the gospel. "But I already know the gospel," you might protest. "I believe Jesus died for my sins and that I have his perfect record, his righteousness, not my own. Why review the basics here?"

Why? Because the gospel will give us the strength to engage cross-culturally, to examine our own areas of sin and blindness, and to persevere when this is uncomfortable. The gospel tells me that I'm more sinful and broken than I can dare admit; yet more loved, forgiven, and made righteous in Christ than I ever dared hope.

We embrace our status as both sanctified and sinner, what Martin Luther called simul justus et peccator.

> **The gospel gives us the strength to engage cross-culturally, to examine our own sin and blindness, and to persevere.**

The African American lawyer, the Caucasian food service worker, the Latin American refugee, and the Korean stay-at-home parent all stand on equal footing before the cross. The pastor, the plumber, and the parking valet are welcomed into the Kingdom of God based on the atoning work of Jesus.

Our capacity for ministry—for serving others—depends on our capacity for suffering. The gospel enables us to suffer with hope, or to suffer redemptively. We can persevere, reflecting the unconditional love we have received. We can forgive those who wound us and ask others for forgiveness. Unconditional love can't be faked. Either gospel grace flows out of us—or it doesn't.

As we massage the gospel deeper into our hearts, we let go of our need to be right. We don't have to hide our failures, earn our way to heaven, or prove how "good" we are. We don't have to master our to-do lists. We don't have to justify ourselves. Why? Because we are 100% forgiven and 100% justified ("just as if I'd never sinned") by faith in Christ.

> **Our capacity for ministry depends on our capacity for suffering. Only as we are grounded in the gospel can we suffer redemptively.**

> Who shall bring any charge against God's elect? It is God who justifies. Who is to condemn? Christ Jesus is the one who died—more than that, who was raised—who is at the right hand of God, who indeed is interceding for us. (Rom. 8:33-34)

Jesus lived the life we should have lived, died the death we should have died, was raised to life so that through his substitutionary work on our behalf we too may be raised to new life, both now and eternally. Paul triumphally proclaims that nothing can separate us from the love of God in Christ.

Our sanctification—the process of becoming more like

Christ—is also by grace. As we keep in step with the Spirit, we are gradually being transformed and made more like what God intended and declares us to be (Col. 2:6).

Because of the gospel, we are less driven to justify and explain ourselves, to protest that no, of course we're not insensitive or unaware or even—gasp—the "r" word: racist. In *The Happy Christian*, David Murray writes, "The gospel doesn't deny or exploit guilt but deals with it. The gospel humbles both White supremacy and Black power. The gospel gives vengeance over to God. The gospel replaces hate with love. The gospel gives powerful hope."[1]

HISTORY WINDOW 2

Enslavement in the Colonies Begins

Bondage is as old as history; slavery is mentioned in the Bible, and the Greeks, Romans, the Islamic world, and the Ottoman empire all included enslavement. It persists and prospers even today in a world marked by sin. Astonishingly, "At the end of the eighteenth century, well over three-quarters of all people alive were in bondage [in]… various systems of slavery or serfdom."[2]

In most cultures, slavery was a result of capture in war or being sold to pay one's debts. The enslaved were not born into servitude and had some rights. Enslavement was not based on race or ethnic origin. In contrast, America's race-based, chattel system, which considered the enslaved as personal property, became particularly pernicious.

The Portuguese initiated the Atlantic slave trade in 1444, importing the first large number of captured and enslaved Africans to Europe. In 1526, Spanish explorers brought enslaved Africans to their settlements in North America.[3]

In 1619, a Dutch ship that had seized "cargo" from a Portuguese slaving ship sold a group of Africans to the colonists. Since indentured servanthood existed in the colonies, these men and women may have been purchased as such. Bound by contracts for a period of time, indentured servants were provided food and housing, and after fulfilling their contract were paid "freedom dues." Initially, indentured Africans and Whites were treated equally and frequently lived and worked together. Colonial records indicate that some Africans lived as free people, owning land and buying their own indentured African servants. But the noose of slavery would soon tighten.

Chapter 3

The Gospel Unites Us

United in the Gospel

Many years ago, the pastor of a church I'll call Grace Hill phoned my husband. "I recommended your church to some folks who visited here. I told Charles and Jackie they'd probably be more comfortable at Faith."

"Great," Craig said. "I look forward to meeting them. Tell me more."

Craig learned that this couple lived closer to Grace Hill than to Faith. Why would they be "more comfortable" driving an extra thirty minutes to attend our church?

Because they were African American.

Grace Hill Church was Caucasian. Our church was multiethnic. How had Charles and Jackie viewed this pastor's remark? People often feel uncomfortable as the sole member of their race in a setting; had they taken this risk, and then been made to feel unwelcome?

Ironically, the area around Grace Hill was transitioning from largely White to primarily Black. What could have helped that pastor and the people of Grace Hill to be more welcoming? To feel more equipped to minister cross-culturally?

Little has changed since the Rev. Dr. Martin Luther King Jr. called 11 o'clock on Sunday morning "the most segregated hour of Christian America." Most churches do not reflect the demographics of their increasingly diverse communities. A 2013 Lifeway Research study found that although 85% of pastors said every church should strive for racial diversity, 86% said their congregation was predominantly one racial or ethnic group. While multiethnic churches have been increasing among evangelicals, fewer than one in four are diverse (with at least 20% of its attendees from different racial or ethnic groups).

America's changing demographics hammer home the realization that churches must learn to welcome their multiethnic neighbors. In 2019, the United States was 60% White. But according to recent census data, by 2045, the U.S. will be "minority White." Estimates are that 25% of Americans will be Hispanic, 14% Asian, and 13% Black. Minorities are now the majority in Texas, Hawaii, New Mexico, and California.

Churches that can't effectively reach across racial and ethnic divides will stagnate.

> **Churches that can't effectively reach across racial and ethnic divides will stagnate or close their doors.**

Some will close their doors altogether. Millennials and Gen Z—who are now the largest generations of Americans and the most racially and ethnically diverse generation in the country—are choosing to stay away from church in droves.

Being part of a racially, ethnically, and socio-economically diverse church has enriched my life in immeasurable ways. As I hear my African American friends tell of being stopped by police because they "looked like somebody" or being passed over for promotions because "you'll never be the face of this institution," I know racism is still a problem. Friends who struggle financially help me realize I don't need so much stuff. I've watched immigrant friends haltingly speak their new language and see people react with impatience or scorn. My Japanese-American friend, a lawyer, is often questioned about where she's from and why she speaks such good English. A Korean friend was beaten up repeatedly by schoolmates when he first arrived in Baltimore and called "Jackie Chan" (Chan is Chinese). My Sri Lankan friend Sahayini is still occasionally rejected by patients who want "an American doctor." Tashmima had been a teacher in Bangladesh but had to support her daughters by working at a convenience store in America.

Many leaders and congregations want their churches to reflect God's heart for all people. They want people from different ethnic and racial groups to feel welcome. But how? What issues need to be addressed? How might we be inadvertently setting up barriers that exclude people from other ethnicities or races?

We start with the theological underpinnings: what we believe should guide how we act. God's plan to reach all nations with the gospel and create one unified body of beloved believers is clear

> God's plan to reach all nations with the gospel and create one unified body of beloved believers is clear from Genesis to Revelation.

from Genesis to Revelation. The Old Testament is infused with God's plan to bless and gather believers from "all nations" and his concern for the foreigner and the immigrant. In the New Testament, Jesus confronts ethnocentric prejudices, intentionally travels to diverse, Gentile-populated regions, and performs miracles for non-Jewish followers.

Once you see this in the Scriptures, you can't unsee it. Awareness of God's plan for beautiful diversity adds new depth to Bible reading and provides fresh insights to familiar stories. We will explore many of these passages in this study.

A Deeper Dive: God's Plan to Reach All Peoples

Israel was fertile territory for God's message of salvation for all peoples. This small nation served as an important land bridge connecting Asia, Africa, and the East. Because of this, ancient empires invaded again and again, intent on controlling important trade routes: Assyria, Babylon, Persia, Greece, Rome.

God promised Abraham that through his offspring "all nations of the earth shall be blessed" (Gen. 18:18; Gen. 26:2, 4). He repeated this message through the prophets. Through Isaiah, God promised that he will accept all those who love him and who adhere to his covenant. "These I will bring to my holy mountain, and make them joyful in my house of prayer." Rather than being the temple of a tribal deity who only accepts Israelites, he said, "My house will be called a house of prayer for all peoples" (Isa. 56:7).

As Jesus began his ministry, he moved to Capernaum, a more diverse area close to the international trade route. Descendants of Abraham lived side by side with non-Jews in this area, sometimes intermarrying with them. Jesus's first sermon in his hometown synagogue in Nazareth underscored his inclusive message—and met with fierce resistance. (Luke 4:16-30) When Jesus read from Isaiah and applied the prophecy to himself, the townspeople were thrilled. But when he confronted their ethnocentric prejudices, the mood shifted: he reminded them that God sent Elijah to help a Phoenician widow in Zarephath rather than famine-struck Israelites, and that Elisha did not heal Israelite lepers but only Naaman, a Syrian conqueror. Infuriated, the people tried to throw Jesus off a cliff.

Most Bible scholars believe Jesus cleansed the temple both at the beginning and end of his ministry to illustrate his zeal for God's holiness and his desire that worship be accessible to all nations (Mark 11:15-18; John 2:13-17). The temple included an area specifically for non-Jews, but commerce had co-opted this Court of the Gentiles. Rather than a sacred space for foreigners to worship, it had become a mall for merchants, with sheep bleating, pigeons flapping, and coins clinking. Rather than the aroma of incense, the stench of animal dung lingered. God's designated space for foreigners had been compromised.

This was such a distortion of God's vision that Jesus made a whip, drove out livestock, turned over tables, and scattered coins. His actions weren't a sudden outburst or temper tantrum (Mark tells us Jesus had visited the temple the day before), but a planned, prophetic demonstration. This story affirms God's desire to welcome all nations. It also foreshadowed Jesus's role as the Lamb of God who bears our sins.

As Jesus moved toward the cross, his desire to reach all nations became even clearer. After Palm Sunday, some Greek pilgrims in Jerusalem asked the disciple Philip if they could see Jesus. (Philip is a Greek name, and he may have been a link to the Greco-Jewish community.) When this request reached Jesus, he announced that the fulfillment of his mission was upon them. "The hour has come for the Son of Man to be glorified. Truly, truly I say to you, unless a grain of wheat falls into the earth and dies, it remains alone; but if it dies, it bears much fruit" (John 12:23-26).

God had revealed his plan to redeem people from every tribe, nation, and tongue in his Word and in Jesus. This came into even sharper focus after the Resurrection. The early church grappled with Christianity's transition from a largely Jewish sect to a movement to reach all peoples "to the ends of the earth."

HISTORY WINDOW 3

Early Contact with Native Americans: Enslavement and Death

An exhaustive study of the injustices against First Nations is beyond our scope here; suffice it to say that the European "discovery" of North America was catastrophic for Native inhabitants who had lived here for many generations. Eventually, millions of Native people would die from contact with the Old World; disease, war, abuse, and forced removal killed an estimated 90% of the indigenous population.[4] In its quest for land or gold, the U.S. government forcibly removed Native inhabitants from their ancestral homelands and broke treaties with abandon.

New World chattel slavery began in 1493 with Columbus's enslavement of the peaceful Taino on the Caribbean island he called Hispaniola. Rather than protest this injustice, the Catholic Church gave its stamp of approval: Pope Alexander VI declared that Spanish and Portuguese colonists had the right to colonize, convert, and enslave Natives and Africans. Abuse in Spanish colonies was so rampant by the sixteenth century that Bartolome de las Casas, a Spanish friar who advocated for native rights, was appointed "Protector of the Indians."[5] But this was too late for the nearly 7 million Taino who had died. Pope Paul III issued a proclamation (in 1537) opposing enslavement of Indigenous peoples, but many conquistadors ignored it.

Because Native people lacked immunity to European viruses and bacteria, epidemics of smallpox, diphtheria, yellow fever, influenza, and other diseases swept across North America, Mesoamerica, and South America. This, and the ability of First Nations peoples to escape their captors, led early colonists to look to Africa for free labor.

Disease, cultural clashes, greed, and the ever-expanding lust for land continued to kill or displace Native Americans for hundreds of years. Christians largely accepted the notion that God had given North America to White settlers. Most Whites considered Native peoples less "civilized." However, notable exceptions to the disregard for Native peoples include theologian Jonathan Edwards and missionary David Brainerd, who rode thousands of miles on horseback to take the gospel to Native Americans in New England, contributing to his premature death in 1747 at age 29.

Chapter 4

Jesus, The Barrier Breaker

A Uniting Savior, Diverse Friendships

Several years ago, after presenting a workshop downtown, I couldn't find my car. I'd remembered exiting an underground garage through a nondescript office building and glancing at the nearest cross streets so that I could find my way back. But when I retraced my steps, I grew increasingly confused. Had I misremembered? Not walked far enough? I roamed steaming streets for more than an hour. My feet, unaccustomed to long hikes in high heels, sprouted blisters, and I took them off. My crisp "look-your-best-because-you're-presenting" blouse was stained with sweat. I fretted about being late to pick up my daughter from daycare. The fact that I knew what space I'd parked in was little comfort. I berated myself. "Who loses an entire parking garage?"

Finally, I walked into a local nonprofit and confessed my situation. The employees pulled out a map, pointed to possible underground garages based on my description, and offered to drive me around. But then, as if by divine summons, a long-time church member walked by.

"Jim!" I called. As we hugged like old friends, the staffer looked on curiously. Why was this professionally-dressed White lady hugging an African American man in paint-splattered overalls and work boots? "This is Jim," I explained. "He goes to my church!" Gracious friend that he is, Jim volunteered to drive me around in his truck and reunite me with my car.

Sometimes people are visibly curious when diverse groups from my church eat out together. "How do you all know each other? Do you work together?" waitresses ask. After all, what could a young Korean guy, a middle-aged African American woman, a balding White guy, and the thirty-something Latina have in common?

We have Jesus in common.

The decades-old fellowship I've enjoyed with Jim and others from different ethnic, racial, or socioeconomic backgrounds is, sadly, too rare. Most churches struggle to embrace the diversity around them. Ed Stetzer, former executive director of LifeWay Research and executive director of the Billy Graham Center at Wheaton College, said, "Surprisingly, most churchgoers are content with the ethnic status quo in their churches. In a world where our culture is increasingly diverse … it appears most people are happy where they are—and with whom they are. Yet, it's hard for Christians to say they are united in Christ when they are congregating separately."[1]

Jesus reconciles us to God, but also to one another. As part of God's diverse "beloved community," our adoption as sons and daughters becomes primary, superseding other identities. When Paul told the Galatians that there was neither Jew nor Greek, slave nor free, male or female, "for you are all one in Christ Jesus" (Gal. 3:28), he was not erasing gender or ethnic distinctions; he was highlighting believers' surpassing unity. Paul describes it as a "mystery" that once-estranged groups are now "members of the same body" (Eph. 3:6). Just as a nonbiological child is adopted and enfolded into a family, we are adopted into God's diverse family.

Jesus broke down the barriers that separated me from Jim. Our race, background, jobs, and gender were secondary compared to our status as brother and sister in Christ. Because we worshipped together, I knew him. I appreciated his gentle personality, musical talent, practical skills, and his willingness to serve others. And, after he reunited me with my car, I appreciated his sense of direction.

A Deeper Dive: Jesus, Our Model

The community that Jesus formed broke down gender, social, religious, political, ethnic, and class barriers. He intentionally engaged with Gentiles. He taught women, had female disciples, and used women to spread his message. He broke social and religious barriers by eating and drinking with "sinners" and touching lepers and others considered ritually unclean. Observers must have marveled at the diversity of his disciples, who included a Zealot—one who wanted to overthrow Rome—and a tax collector, who collaborated with the occupying force. His followers included the rich and those who eked by in working-class trades.

Most of Jesus's teaching and miracles took place in Galilee, a largely Jewish region located near an important international trade route. This fulfilled Isaiah's prophecy that a light would dawn for "Galilee of the Gentiles."

Jesus surprised his disciples by deliberately taking them to Samaria, Phoenicia, and the Decapolis—more diverse, sometimes even hostile areas. These trips were "geographically exceptional and purposeful."[2]

Bible scholar Jack Beck writes, "Jesus went to these Gentile places to redeem the lost and demonstrate that the Kingdom of God is larger than many considered it to be in the Jewish orbit of the first century."[3]

Although Sychar (originally called Shechem) was the exact spot where the Lord had appeared to Abraham centuries earlier (Gen. 12:1-8), Israelites who lived there had turned from the Lord to worship idols and intermarry with non-Jews. Many Jews reviled Samaritans as impure and considered their worship polluted. Breaking multiple Jewish taboos, Jesus asked a Samaritan woman for water and engaged her in spiritual conversation. He cut through her cultural and religious arguments and revealed his messiahship to her.

> The community Jesus formed broke down gender, social, religious, political, ethic and class barriers.

In Phoenicia (also known as Canaan), in northern Israel, Jesus proved his messiahship with miracles. Jews despised Phoenicians because their ancestors (including Queen Jezebel of 1 Kings 16) had embraced Baal worship and oppressed the Israelites (Joel 3). Here, in Tyre and Sidon, a Canaanite woman asked Jesus to heal her daughter. He drew her out, granted her request, and commended her faith.

Jesus intentionally traveled from the more Jewish, western side of the Sea of Galilee to the eastern side—the Decapolis, Greek for "ten cities." These cities showcased Roman power and superiority, boasting Greco-Roman infrastructure and architecture that included shopping centers, horse-racing stadiums, and hot baths. There he exorcised a man possessed by multiple demons. The demons then entered a herd of pigs who ran off the cliff. (Jews didn't eat pork, but Gentiles did.) Although the man begged to go with Jesus (Luke 8:26-38), the Lord told him to go home and "tell how much God has done for you." News of this miracle spread throughout the Decapolis; some scholars call this man the first apostle to the Gentiles (Mark 5:1-20; Matt. 8:28-34).

When Jesus returned to this region later, crowds flocked to hear him and lingered for three days. Jesus multiplied loaves and fish to feed 4,000 men, plus women and children (Mark 8:1-10). The disciples picked up seven baskets of leftover bread. This event is distinct from the feeding of the 5,000, which happened in a more Jewish area and yielded twelve baskets of leftover loaves. (In the Bible, seven is associated with completeness; God created all humanity in seven days. Twelve represents the twelve tribes of Israel.)

By traveling to ethnically diverse regions, Jesus modeled the behavior he wanted his disciples to follow after his resurrection and ascension. Unlike the scribes and Pharisees, who taught that only ethnic Israel would be saved, Jesus pursued non-Jewish followers and commended them for their faith. His disciples were to go "to the ends of the earth." His intentional ministry to those outside the Jewish mainstream proved he had come so "that my salvation may reach to the end of the earth" (Isa. 49:6).

HISTORY WINDOW 4

Race-Based Slavery in the Colonies

Historian Edward Baptist writes, "The idea that the commodification and suffering and forced labor of African Americans is what made the United States powerful and rich is not an idea that people necessarily are happy to hear. Yet it is the truth.... Enslaved African Americans built the modern United States, and indeed the entire modern world, in ways both obvious and hidden."[6]

This perspective may seem shocking or overblown at first. Yet over the last twenty years, new scholarship has underscored this fact. "At the outbreak of the Civil War, the financial value of enslaved people was higher than the value of railroads, banks, and factories combined."[7] How did we get there?

In colonial America, the concept of race as a determinate of status was not yet fixed. People were not "White"; they were British, Dutch, or Portuguese. "Exploitation came first, and then the ideology of unequal races to justify this exploitation followed."[8] Because the European colonies became dependent on slave labor, especially in the tobacco fields that ensured Virginia's sustainability, an institutionalized race-based slavery evolved, piece by piece, law by law.

In the mid-seventeenth century, colonial lawmakers developed "slave codes." For example, while British law determined that a child's status as free or enslaved depended on that of the father, new colonial laws determined a child's freedom status based on the mother. This made it profitable for slave owners to systematically rape enslaved women to increase their "property."

The response of colonial Christians to this evolving slave system is mixed at best. While the institutional church generally supported evangelizing enslaved Africans, their conversion posed an ethical quandary because British law forbade enslaving Christians. The 1667 Virginia General Assembly eased White consciences by declaring that "baptism does not alter the condition of the person as to his bondage or freedom."

The preaching of Jonathan Edwards, George Whitfield, and others during the First Great Awakening (1730-1740) did not confront the injustice of slavery. Spiritual equality before God did not translate into social equality. While Whitfield criticized cruelty in slave owners, both he and Edwards owned enslaved people. Some congregations welcomed Black worshippers, but almost always with segregated seating. The roots of racial prejudice would spread deep and wide, even in the church.

Chapter 5

Culture and God's Story of Grace
Culture, Creation, and Collards

When my dear friend Cora died unexpectedly, I wanted to pay my respects. The funeral and repast would take place at her church, which I'd never visited. I soon learned that although our hearts had been in sync, our church cultures weren't.

At Faith, many funeral repasts were potluck affairs, so I decided to bring a side dish to Cora's service. I'd lately been eating collard greens—a healthy, cheap staple of "soul food" cooking. Greens are also unmistakably pungent.

As the service started, I hurried in. Where was the fellowship hall where the repast would be served? I couldn't tug the sleeve of the robed clergyman or pull aside the cross-bearing acolyte processing down the wide center aisle. I couldn't bring the dish into the sanctuary with its soaring ceiling, stained-glass windows, and polished wooden pews. I ditched the CorningWare casserole in a corner of the foyer. It squatted there, odd and out of place.

An hour later, when I returned to the foyer, the distinctive aroma of ham hock and collard greens greeted me. Red-faced, I retrieved the casserole as casually as possible. Its chipped glass lid rattled as I followed the crowd to the repast. Everyone else carried only purses and funeral programs. *Uh oh.*

The fellowship hall was decked out for high tea, with china cups, finger sandwiches, and petit fours. Cloth napkins, gleaming silverware, and tasteful centerpieces broadcast elegance. Nary a covered dish in sight. One woman eyed my dish. "Oh, we won't need that," she said. *Clearly.*

My brief mortification resulted from unfamiliarity with Cora's church culture and its traditions. I didn't know the rules.

Simply put, culture is "the way we do things around here." It includes unwritten rules you may not know until you transgress them.

> The Bible is the love story of God's gracious, relentless pursuit of humankind.

Where do we see culture in the Bible? All humans are made in the image of God and bear his divine stamp: the imago Dei. As his spiritual image-bearers, we reflect our Maker's capacity to create—and we create culture. As Soong-Chan Rah writes in *Many Colors*, "Cultures are ... a sincere, albeit fallen, attempt to reflect God's image through the process of creativity."

God calls Adam to steward the earth: to manage, cultivate, and protect it. He gives Adam the job of naming the animals—a sign of agency and power. He creates Eve and calls her and Adam to live in community and fill the earth (fellowship, interdependence, reproduction). Culture-making has begun.

After the Fall in Genesis 3, that cultural objective remains in play—but with new challenges. Our task is harder because of sin inside and out, and the culture we create will be imperfect. At our worst, we distort, deface, or destroy his image. At our best, as agents of his redemption, we create customs or traditions that reflect some aspect of God's truth, beauty, goodness, and creativity. We cooperate with him in bringing his shalom, his deep, wholistic peace, to people in our broken world.

Cora would have chuckled at my urban multiethnic church vibe in her suburban, high church culture. My collards were out of place among the cucumber sandwiches. Neither cultural expression was bad, nor superior, just different. Both expressed sharing and serving, sustenance amid sorrow. Fondly remembering my friend, I celebrated Cora's entrance into the Kingdom of Heaven with tea, tears, and finger sandwiches.

A Deeper Dive: Culture and God's Story of Grace

The Bible is the love story of God's gracious, relentless pursuit of humankind. Viewing the Bible through the Creation, Fall, Redemption, and Restoration (CFRR) model captures God's work in redemptive history. It answers the deep questions people across all cultures ask: How did it all start? What went wrong? How will it get fixed? How will it all end? We see how the Old Testament points forward to Christ's work of redemption, and the New

Testament shows Jesus accomplishing our salvation. This paradigm provides insights about God, ourselves, and our world.

God's original creation experienced abundance, provision, conflict-free relationships, and unbroken fellowship with God. We were created with these longings for fellowship, for worth or significance, for sustenance, and for safety—all of which God provided in the Garden. Yet this shalom, or deep peace, was shattered in the Fall. We—and all of creation—have been affected by sin (Rom. 3:23, 8:22-23). We could say that our DNA is tainted by sin and brokenness. Even our good deeds generally have underlying selfish motives, even if just our attempt to earn our way into God's favor. The penalty for sin is spiritual and physical death: separation from God in eternity (Rom. 6:23).

Jesus's sacrificial death and resurrection fulfilled God's promise to Adam and Eve that a redeemer would crush evil (Rom. 3:23-25; Gal. 3:13). This began the process of re-creating all things. God calls and deploys his people in this mission of restoration. We "embody the gospel through sacrificial service for the common good, to those in need, and to the poor. God's kingdom will eventually overcome hunger, poverty, and injustice."[1] His kingdom will reach fruition in a new heaven and new earth (Rev. 21:1-5; 22:1-5) so beautiful that we struggle to imagine it (1 Cor. 2:9).

We live in "the now-and-not-yet" period between Jesus's first coming and his second coming. Even though we have the foretaste or "firstfruits" of our redemption, we still experience the effects of the Fall.

As we view our lives through the Creation, Fall, Redemption, and Restoration model, we see how it impacts our view of God, ourselves, others, and the world. We can use this paradigm to evaluate our culture: our business practices, families, sexuality, entertainment, lifestyle, and civic engagement. As redeemed people, we are a "new nation, a holy priesthood, a people belonging to God" (1 Pet. 2:9-10). We are to live as "sojourners and exiles" who reflect God's dominion and shalom in this world.

HISTORY WINDOW 5

The American Revolution

When the colonies rebelled against Great Britain, justice for people of African descent was again thwarted. Though an earlier draft of the Declaration of Independence lambasted Great Britain for the transatlantic slave trade, delegates scuttled this clause because several states objected. The "inalienable rights" that slaveholder Thomas Jefferson penned were not extended to women, Native peoples, or darker-hued Americans. Black Americans fought in the Revolutionary War on both sides, hoping to secure these rights. As many as 20,000 joined the British cause, drawn by the promise of liberation.

The young nation wrestled with slavery but yielded to the seductive lure of wealth and free labor. Fear of financial ruin encouraged moral relativism. Both Southern and Northern capitalism—and even European markets—benefited from slavery, which helped increase shipping, expanded capital, and provided cheap cotton to booming Northern mills.

When the Constitutional Convention of 1787 considered the issue, it capitulated to the demands of pro-slavery factions by including an early fugitive slave clause (another would follow in 1850). It also included the infamous Three-Fifths Clause, which counted an enslaved Black person as three-fifths of a White citizen for purposes of representation.

Chapter 6

Culture, Creation, and Fall

Am I a Racist?

One night, traveling home by Uber, I recognized the driver's accent as we chatted. "Are you from Nigeria?" I asked. When he answered yes, fear clutched my stomach. The week before, I'd wept with a young woman who'd been attacked by a Nigerian acquaintance. My mind raced. In Baltimore, the immigrant community can be close—does this man know the attacker? Is it safe to ride with him?

Was this a racist thought? Does this mean I'm a racist?

Most people bristle at the idea that they might be racist. "I'm colorblind and treat everyone the same!" "We're all God's children." "I'm not racist; I have Black/Asian/Latino friends/coworkers."

Part of the pushback is rooted in how we define racist. The word conjures up hooded Ku Klux Klan men burning crosses, or a lynching tree, or fire hoses spraying protesters in Montgomery,

Alabama, in 1963. Or Dylan Roof executing Black worshippers at a Bible study in Charleston in 2015. We think of egregious racist actions.

Yet racism—the belief that some races are inherently superior—is woven into the fabric of our nation. Racism devalues people based on their physical traits or ethnicity. It may look like overt animosity or passive disregard. Race has been used to establish norms of beauty, behavior, and belonging; for example, elevating "proximity to Whiteness" has led people to want whitening creams or Asian eyelid surgery. Policies have been enacted that use race to determine whether a person could be free, vote, or own property. Race has determined where you could work, who you could marry, and where you could live. In many cases, it has determined whether you live or die.

Rather than seeing racism as "a loathsome character defect," journalist Leonard Pitts Jr. writes, "It's the water in which we swim."[1] Even if I may not consciously devalue or hate people, I function within structures built around principles or preferences that value some people over others. If I deny that this shapes my perspective, I communicate my unwillingness to engage in difficult conversations about race or to listen to the painful racial experiences of people of color. If I fail to speak up when racism appears, I add to the problem.

How should I as a Christian think about racism? Just as I am shaped by other aspects of my culture that do not honor God—overvaluing youth, beauty, or material success, finding my identity in achievements—I am shaped by race-related cultural messages in subtle ways. Although the word "racism" is not in the Bible, the concept of hating or devaluing people based on difference is as old as the Fall. This isn't a White problem; it's a human problem. It's not an American problem, but a global problem. By devaluing the imago Dei, the image of God in every human, racism ultimately rejects God and his authority. It also violates the principle of salvation by grace alone; we can use our race and culture to bolster our sense of significance, security, and worth apart from God. Pointing the finger, however, is a slippery slope because we are all fallen. Finally, racism violates Jesus's commandment to love one's neighbor as oneself.

Theologically, I can admit I'm guilty of racism—just as I am guilty of coveting, unforgiveness, and other failings. I believe in the doctrine of total depravity, which "doesn't mean that all human beings are as wicked as they can possibly be. It means that the Fall was so serious that it affects the whole person."[2] I am an equal-opportunity sinner, capable of exerting my selfish desires against others whether they look like me or not. Yet secure in Christ's love, I can venture into the dark basement of my heart and repent without fearing emotional or spiritual annihilation. The gospel is powerful enough to address my sins, guilt, and denial—including racism. My identity is based not on my goodness, but on Jesus's perfect righteousness credited to me. Because of the cross, I can move from denial to understanding, from despair to hope, from rage to forgiveness. And that is good news.

If I resist the urge to shut down, self-defend, blame-shift, or argue when someone points out my shortcomings—even those I'm unaware of—I cooperate with the Holy Spirit's work of transformation. I become more like Jesus.

Back to my Uber driver. His skin color (the trait most used to define race) when he pinged me with his arrival time

> The gospel is powerful enough to address my sins, guilt and denial—including racism.

had caused me no concern. His accent, however, triggered a memory of a fresh trauma, and I prejudged him based on his country of origin. I defeated my brief irrational fear by remembering Nigerian men and women at church I love and respect. But what if I'd had no Nigerian friends? What if when he'd arrived, I'd crossed my arms and refused to ride with him? In my prejudice, I would have deprived him of a fare. That would be racist. And not loving my neighbor as myself.

A Deeper Dive into Culture, Creation, and Fall

In the Fall, God's original design of unbroken fellowship between humanity and God and humanity and creation were shattered. Our ability to communicate across cultures without causing conflict or misunderstanding (known as cultural intelligence) was damaged. Our "natural man" wants to pursue self-interest even if it disadvantages or oppresses others.

Here are some ways the Fall impacts our thinking, especially in relation to cross-cultural interactions.

1. **We love ourselves above God and others.** We also tend to love those most like us.
2. **We don't want to admit we have sinful prejudices.** We don't want to accept how sinful we are; we resist change; we commit cultural/racial sins of omission as well as commission.
3. **We read the Bible with cultural blinders.** David Livermore, who writes extensively on Christians and culture, says, "Studies examining cultural intelligence among American ministry leaders reveal their subjects' limited awareness of how significantly culture shapes the way one reads the Bible."[3]
4. **We make premature judgments.** People tend to attribute negative characteristics to things that are new and not understood. We equate different with wrong or inadequate.
5. **We misunderstand others.** We are generally unaware of our misconceptions; we don't stop to question whether others see things as we do; we tend to assume everyone else has the same perspective we do.
6. **We lack understanding of our own cultural makeup.** Everyone is culturally biased. To grow, we need to first identify and name our cultural values, then evaluate them biblically, and either affirm or challenge them. For example, is a "white-collar" job more prestigious than a "blue-collar" one? Or, what does it mean to be "on time"?
7. **Westerners have an individualized worldview, not a biblical one.** *Christianity Today* writes that "most white evangelicals deny the existence of any ongoing racial problem in the U.S., and many blame the media and African Americans who refuse to forget the past for any lingering racial conflict. This

perception ... is not so much informed by racism but by a commitment to an individualized theological worldview that blinds many white evangelicals to certain societal injustices." [4]

The Fall is not the final word; Jesus is the final Word. Because of the gospel, we can grow in our ability to cross cultures and minister to others in love, with respect and appreciation for differences.

HISTORY WINDOW 6

Separate-and-Unequal Christianity

The Second Great Awakening (1790-1820) allowed a separate-and-unequal Christianity. It emphasized individual conversion "without a corresponding focus on transforming the racist policies and practices of institutions, a stance that has remained a constant feature of American evangelicalism and has furthered the American church's easy compromise with slavery and racism."[9] Even abolitionist Charles Finney (1792-1875), who excluded White enslavers from church membership, did not believe in Black equality and relegated Black worshippers to a separate section. The first African American denomination, the African Methodist Episcopal Church (AME), was founded in 1816 in Philadelphia by formerly enslaved Richard Allen, after he and other Black worshippers were forcibly excluded from praying in a Whites-only space.

Southern theologians tended to write and preach that slavery was biblical. It emphasized the enslaved peoples' duty to obey their masters (Eph. 6:5; Col. 3:22). Passages that spoke to the equality of all humankind (Col. 3:11; 1 Cor. 12:13; Gal. 3:28), or that directly contradicted or limited slavery, were avoided or even excised from "slave Bibles" (Eph. 6:9; Exod. 21:16; 1 Tim. 1:10; Deut. 24:7). Southern theologians taught that enslaved Africans benefited from contact with the "nobler race" of Whites who introduced them to Christian teaching, even though Christianity had arrived in Africa in the first century; early church fathers from the African continent included Augustine, Tertullian, and Athanasius.

Chapter 7

Culture, Redemption, and Restoration

Becoming Aware of Cultural Dissonance

"Wa' hack?" the teenager asked as I exited the grocery store. New to Baltimore, I couldn't decode his thick accent.

"I'm sorry. What?"

"Wa' a hack?" he repeated, more insistently.

I looked at him dumbly, trying to grasp meaning from context. Did I want something? What might I need as I exited the grocery store? I was clueless.

The store, located a few blocks from the rundown house we were renovating, smelled stale and dirty, an aroma I'd learn to associate with rodent droppings. Its lettuce looked wilted, its fruit wrinkled and bruised. Cashiers seemed bored and unfriendly. And, apparently, I was too ignorant to understand the young men who lingered outside.

"You wa' hack?" the teenager repeated.

I couldn't ask him to repeat it again. I feared he'd feel disrespected. A cultural chasm loomed between us. How to end this, stop my discomfort?

I decided I didn't need whatever he was offering. "Uh, no, thanks." He moved on to another shopper.

Later, I realized he'd asked if I wanted an unlicensed taxi, or hack, to haul my groceries home. Juggling bags of groceries on public transportation is awkward; many shoppers in this neighborhood hire drivers.

Craig and I didn't have to. We owned a car. True, someone had given it to us. We'd moved into a distressed Baltimore neighborhood to start a church that would welcome people from all ethnicities and backgrounds. We hoped and prayed it could be a spiritual home for young men like this. But how could I welcome someone whose accent I couldn't understand?

I began adjusting to Baltimore. I learned about hacks and how to flag them down. I stopped being jarred when strangers called me "hon." I learned a "pockeybook" was a purse, that you washed dishes in the "zinc," and went "downy oshun" for sun and sand. I also learned it's a privilege to own a car or a washing machine.

Over time, I would understand the myriad reasons why more young people in Baltimore dropped out of high school than graduated. How finding a job—and getting to that job on public transportation—was harder than I'd realized. Sure, I'd worked since age 15, but my parents, my background, and my education had prepped me. I'd had the privilege of a family that provided good nutrition, medical and dental care, schooling, and the "soft skills" that helped me show up every day, on time, healthy and ready to work.

I'd heard of culture shock but hadn't applied it to my urban experience. With no training for my new ministry role, a year after our marriage, I was raising a newborn, helping renovate our house, and serving as our fledgling church's volunteer secretary, musician, and nursery coordinator.

Eight years after moving to Baltimore, I attended a seminar on urban ministry taught by theologian Dr. Harvie Conn, where he talked about culture shock. He described stopping by the 7-Eleven in his Philadelphia neighborhood and waiting in line when a brawl broke out. Insults flew, one shopper shoved another, and Dr. Conn's jug of milk was knocked out of his hand, arced up then down, and exploded on the floor. He wondered if someone might pull a gun, so he left without the milk. And this was, somehow, not unusual.

Yes! I thought. Dr. Conn had given words to my experience and normalized the cultural dissonance I felt but couldn't articulate. I was exhausted from the stress of four children under seven, an overworking husband, and church crises that were exacerbated by cross-cultural tensions. I started to cry, and much to my chagrin, couldn't make myself stop.

Cultural dissonance can be a wise teacher. Only when I crossed cultures did I understand I had a culture: White, middle-class, third-generation descendant of European immigrants. I'd absorbed culture from parents: the right way to do things. Set the table properly. Clean your plate. Don't belch. Dinner consisted of meat, a starch (usually potatoes), and a vegetable, followed by a dessert. Don't answer the phone during meals.

These are all culturally determined. Does setting the table look like *Downton Abbey* or a single pot in the middle of the floor? In some cultures, it's rude to finish everything on your plate and a compliment to burp. Some cultures believe it's disrespectful to look an older person in the eye, while I had learned to greet people by shaking hands and making eye contact. Millions of people build their meals around rice and beans, with nary a potato in sight.

Regardless of our culture, race, or background, we are equal at the foot of the cross. As we interact with other cultures, we can view our convictions, habits, and presuppositions with fresh eyes. For example, is my preferred worship style a biblical principle or just a personal preference? Do I interpret the commandment to "honor your father and mother" differently from believers in other cultures? What does my culture consider modest attire?

Entering into another's world may unsettle or upend our deeply held convictions. We may feel ignorant or foolish, or excited and invigorated. This challenge exercises muscles of humility, curiosity, and resilience. It requires intention and a willingness to learn, make mistakes, and persevere. The end result? We grow in Christlikeness. And we are dramatically richer for the experience.

A Deeper Dive: How God Redeems and Restores Culture

Looking at culture—and the dissonance or disorientation we may feel interacting with other cultures—through the lens of Creation, Fall, Redemption, and Restoration helps us appreciate God's grace. We see the beauty of God's diverse creation, but also how it is damaged in the Fall. Redemption unites God's diverse people as part of God's universal family, and points forward to the day when God will restore all things.

This ultimate restoration is not a whitewashed, personality-erasing, melding-into-the-universal-oneness; we retain our individual characteristics.

In *The Beautiful Community*, Dr. Irwyn Ince writes, "The Spirit does not remove our diversity. Rather he enables us to love, hear, seek, understand, and pursue one another in our diversity. ... The Fall destroyed union and unity with God and each other. Reunion is the story of Scripture."[1]

> The ultimate Restoration is not a whitewashed, personality-erasing, melding-into-the-universal-oneness; we retain our individual characteristics.

At this ultimate family reunion, we retain our unique differences. Theologian Esau McCaulley writes:

These distinct peoples, cultures, and languages are eschatological, everlasting. ... God's eschatological vision for the reconciliation of all things in his Son requires my blackness and my neighbor's Latina identity to endure forever. ... Our distinctive cultures represent the means by which we give honor to God. He is honored through the diversity of tongues singing the same song.[2]

We will not be colorblind in heaven and should not pretend to be now. People sometimes protest, "I'm not prejudiced. I don't see race." Yet this is disingenuous, stemming from a fear of being accused of racism. We do notice race, and gender, and dozens of other details about other people. Imagine how insulted a man would be if I said, "I don't see you as a guy. I don't notice gender." Or if I commented, "You say you've lost 50 pounds this year? Gosh, I didn't notice. I don't see body type."

The notion of color blindness "is sub-biblical and falls short of the glory of God."[3] Revelation 7 reveals the vision of "a great multitude that no one could count, from every nation, tribe, people, and language, standing before the throne and before the Lamb" worshipping together. Imagine the beautiful cacophony! The variety! The costumes, languages, and skin tones! To God be the glory.

HISTORY WINDOW 7

The New Nation: Marked with the Sin of Slavery

As the new nation wrestled with slavery and its expansion, lawmakers attempted to stitch the strained nation back together, or at least postpone the inevitable split. As foment between pro- and anti-slavery factions increased, most laws protected and expanded slavery. One notable exception was the 1808 law banning the transatlantic slave trade. However, this law was poorly funded or enforced and failed to stop the lucrative trade.

U.S. traffickers drew on America's diplomatic strength, shipbuilding, and investment capital to sustain the trade. Baltimore led the way in producing large, fast vessels that eluded lackluster anti-trafficking patrols, and New York City, a shipping and financial center, was "an especially attractive hub for the traffickers. ... The United States, therefore, was in many ways the linchpin in the triangular route."[10]

In the 1830s and 1840's, additional southeastern and southwestern lands—after being largely purged of Native Americans— opened up to settlers who embraced slavery. Cotton plantations—what historians today call slave labor camps—sprouted in present-day Mississippi, Alabama, Louisiana, and eventually Texas. Coffles of chained, enslaved people were marched hundreds of miles to work in them.

The Fugitive Slave Act (1850) criminalized helping the runaway slaves and further endangered free Black men, women, and children in the North who were captured and "returned" South in the "reverse Underground Railroad." It also forced those fleeing slavery to travel all the way to Canada.

The Missouri Compromise (1820) had guaranteed that the "peculiar institution" would flourish not only in Missouri but in some new states as well. But in 1854, the Kansas-Nebraska Act repealed this compromise, and left the decision to enter the Union as free or enslaved with the states themselves. This resulted in the sectional bloodshed of "Bleeding Kansas." The Dred Scott Decision (1857) classified African Americans as "an inferior order," denying them the rights of citizens.

By the late 1850s, America had reached a boiling point. The fiery, violent abolitionist John Brown came to believe that "moral persuasion is hopeless" and raided the federal armory in Harper's Ferry, Virginia, to spearhead a slave rebellion. Convicted of murder and treason in 1859, his final words included, "I am now quite certain that the crimes of this guilty land will never be purged away, but with blood." The Civil War erupted a year later.

Chapter 8

The Early Church Meets Culture
Culture Eats Strategy

In high school, our oldest daughter Rebecca attended an expensive private school on scholarship. Baltimore boasts many such schools, and after moving here, I learned that when adults ask, "Where did you go to school?" they don't mean college. They mean high school. This factoid often signals your family background and socioeconomic status. Did you attend a public school, an elite private school, or one of the Catholic or Lutheran schools that draw students from more diverse backgrounds?

We hoped Rebecca would connect with a Christian organization that had a chapter at her school. Craig's high school involvement in Young Life, a Christian youth organization, had been spiritually transforming. The group at her school was similar to Young Life, with chapters at private schools nationwide. Craig and I decided to attend the information session for parents.

I often felt out of place at her school meetings, where most parents seemed to have high-profile jobs and hefty salaries. Being a curriculum writer married to a pastor in the 'hood hardly carried any social cachet and necessitated a far more frugal lifestyle. At times, I felt the socioeconomic gap keenly. Had I dressed appropriately? Did our clothes look like they came from Goodwill?

Craig and I took seats at one of the large plastic folding tables. Some parents knew each other and chatted easily. We nodded and smiled at others, but no one greeted us personally. As the tables began to fill, a woman in stylish business attire approached us.

"Would you mind moving to another table?" she said. "My friends and I always sit at this one."

The tables were identical. Plenty of other seats were available. We're all creatures of habit, but I would never have asked someone to vacate "my" pew at church so that I could sit in my usual spot. As a newcomer, I felt unwelcome. *Strike one.*

We smiled and moved. The woman thanked us, and her friends moved over to "her" table. I raised my eyebrows at Craig.

After the meeting, another woman introduced herself. She peppered us with questions about our student. Did she like the school? Was she interested in the club? What church did we go to? I started to relax into the conversation. Then came the question that was often problematic at this school.

"Where do you live?"

I hedged my response, naming the larger community that included a mix of neighborhoods. "Govans," I answered.

"Oh, I know Govans," she said. "Where in Govans?" *Here it comes,* I thought. "We live in Pen Lucy."

She gasped. "My maid lives in Pen Lucy!" She named the street.

"Yes, we live just a few blocks from there."

She looked at me, flummoxed. The conversation flagged. I felt even more like an outsider who didn't belong. *Strike two.*

When we returned home, Rebecca asked about the meeting. Though we laughed off the "my maid lives in Pen Lucy" remark, she was adamant. "I'm not going to that club." *Strike three.*

The women at the meeting had difficulty stepping outside their cultural comfort zone, whether it was sitting at "their" table or understanding that some White people live in primarily Black neighborhoods. They didn't adjust their actions or words to be more intentionally welcoming; they defaulted to what felt familiar.

It's said that "culture eats strategy" because we tend to default to our culture—what feels "normal" to us, what we do without thinking. I returned home convinced of two things: one, my daughter, sadly, would not want to connect to that group; and two, I vowed to redouble my efforts to welcome the new person or the outsider.

The Early Church Meets Culture

God's original mission to bless all nations through Abraham and his descendants had often been sidelined. Although Jesus had demonstrated in both word and deed his inclusive kingdom, his disciples had been steeped in generations of belief in "Jewish exclusivity" as God's chosen people. Rather than seeing themselves as a light to the Gentiles, many Jews longed for a liberating

Messiah to rescue them from conquering empires and restore their political glory. Jesus cracked open this paradigm. This Messiah's kingdom was grander than a political empire or second Davidic golden age; it transcended Israel to embrace the whole world.

When the Church was birthed at Pentecost (Acts 2), believers had to learn new theology to integrate members from different cultural and religious backgrounds. The nations had been scattered at the Tower of Babel, but God began reuniting them, pouring out his Holy Spirit so that pilgrims from many regions heard "in our own tongues the mighty works of God."

As people from all nations and classes became Jesus-followers, some leaders were confused or resistant. They needed to evaluate their cultural practices and traditions in light of this new, expanded Kingdom of God.

When the apostles initially faced the practical implications of a cross-cultural gospel, they stumbled.

As they distributed food to impoverished widows (Acts 6:1-7), they inadvertently overlooked the Greek-speaking women. When this was brought to their attention, they didn't ignore these powerless women. They didn't say, "These women are culturally

> As people from all nations and classes became Jesus-followers, leaders needed to evaluate their cultural practices in light of this new, expanded Kingdom of God.

different and speak another language; let's split into two groups." They appointed a diverse leadership team of qualified Greek-speaking leaders to care for these widows. They preserved the unity of the church.

God continued to push the boundaries of his church, miraculously plucking the Apostle Philip out of Jerusalem to evangelize a prominent Ethiopian pilgrim. Philip showed the Ethiopian eunuch that Jesus was the "suffering servant" foretold by Isaiah and baptized him (Acts 8:26-40). This encounter underscores not only the inclusive nature of God's kingdom, but the fact that Africans are "at the beginning of the emerging Christian community."[1]

God supernaturally directed Peter to Cornelius, a devout God-fearing Roman. God showed Peter a vision of "unclean" Gentile foods and instructed him to eat, upending Jewish dietary restrictions (Acts 10). God had to show Peter the vision three times before it sank in. Dr. Irwyn Ince writes, "Peter stands in need of some radical theological correction. … The new normal in Jesus Christ did not mean having to conform to ethnic Jewish life. … Faith in Jesus Christ has replaced overt exclusion with radical inclusion."[2] Jesus had broken down the dividing walls and united Jew and Gentile.

Jesus commissioned Paul as an apostle to the Gentiles. As Paul preached across the Mediterranean world, the "other" became a brother or sister in the faith. Similarly, when the Apostle Peter reported back on his Gentile encounters, the other believers were "astonished" that the Holy Spirit had been poured out on them (Acts 10:45).

Through these examples and others, we see that what had begun as a Jewish sect in a tiny, Middle Eastern nation was becoming a global, multiethnic movement. As the gospel spread, its leaders grappled with wrenching questions. Do we still follow the Jewish traditions? What about circumcision and dietary laws? And ultimately, what does it mean to be a follower of Jesus? Over time, God's unifying gospel became clearer. Through the power and leading of the Holy Spirit, Gentiles were enfolded, the poor cared for, and the Kingdom of God advanced.

How does this relate to the racial, ethnic, and cultural diversity we face today? Like the apostles, we tend to revert to our familiar cultural expressions. Because Caucasians have historically been the dominant culture in the United States, White culture is often internalized as "normal." We often don't realize this until something or someone interrupts that presupposition. Because of this, the first step in developing cross-cultural awareness, becoming more welcoming to others, and experiencing this unifying power of the gospel is to examine our own culture. Keep reading to learn more.

HISTORY WINDOW 8

Abolition

By the late 1700s, abolitionism was gaining momentum globally, often driven by Christian beliefs. Twelve men gathered in a London print shop in 1787 to found the Society for the Abolition of the Slave Trade. "All of the twelve were deeply religious, and the twenty-seven-year-old [Thomas] Clarkson wore black clerical garb,"[11] writes Adam Hochschield. Great Britain banned the slave trade in 1807, and in 1833 outlawed slavery in its empire. In 1780, Pennsylvania passed a gradual emancipation law, and Massachusetts' constitution declared all men equal.

Conflict over America's chattel slavery system roiled American Christians. Even without the transatlantic trade, "natural increase"--boosted by White masters raping and impregnating enslaved women—supplied America's lust for free labor. Enslaved women's value was linked not just to their work capacity but to their fertility and attractiveness based on White criteria of beauty (i.e., lighter skin tone). Recent DNA research reveals that nearly all African Americans have some European ancestry which entered the gene pool before the Civil War—hardly a time of consensual interracial relationships.[13] Did the church turn a blind eye to the presence of lighter-hued children who were the offspring of White owners? Were adultery and theft of labor and lives omitted from the Ten Commandments? Arguments over enslavement caused sectional splits in several denominations.

Yet even as slavery expanded, pushback grew, especially from Christians. The writings of Rev. John Rankin (b. 1793) influenced other prominent abolitionists including William Lloyd Garrison, Theodore Weld, and Rev. Henry Ward Beecher. Though they differed on how to end slavery and deal with the formerly enslaved, most abolitionists agreed that slavery was sin. One early casualty was Presbyterian minister and abolitionist Elijah Lovejoy in Alton, Illinois, martyred in 1837 by a pro-slavery mob intent on demolishing his printing press.

By the 1840s, thousands of abolitionists had joined anti-slavery societies.[15] Black voices included Henry Highland Garnet, Sojourner Truth, Harriet Tubman, and the authors of compelling slave narratives, such as Frederick Douglass and Harriet Jacobs. Harriet Beecher Stowe's *Uncle Tom's Cabin* (1852) wrung the hearts of readers at home and abroad as it portrayed how slavery dehumanized Blacks and debased Whites. Stowe believed that "there is more done with pens than with swords," but the time for swords had come.

Chapter 9

How Diversity Benefits The Church
How Diversity Benefited My Kids

"Shame on you, Craig Garriott, for moving your family into the city!"

The woman who scolded Craig articulated what others expressed more obliquely. Was it wise to raise our kids in a lower-income minority neighborhood? For the next twenty-two years, as we raised five children two blocks from where Craig pastored our multiethnic church, we asked ourselves: Had we heard God correctly? Were we damaging our kids? Now that our kids are adults, we have the benefit of hindsight. While life was difficult at times, they are thankful for where they were raised.

We stood out, whether we wanted to or not. We were college graduates in a neighborhood where more than half didn't finish high school, homeowners on a street where 70% of the houses were rentals. We owned a car and didn't have to depend on public transportation. Our kids didn't attend the neighborhood schools.

We felt the weight of America's painful racial history. We were the only Whites on our street and one of a handful of White families in the community. When we first renovated our house, neighbors asked, "When will the apartments be ready?" Aware of the "White savior" complex, we came as participants and learners. And learn we did.

> If we limit the gospel's message to individual reconciliation with God, we truncate it.

Our neighborhood struggled with joblessness, violence, low-performing schools, and crime. Our kids saw that poverty creates a lack of good choices. Your neighborhood school has rock-bottom test scores? Too bad—you can't afford another option. Need money for your cell phone bill or to help Mom but can't find an after-school job? The dealers are hiring. Need training to get out of your low-wage job but can't afford tuition? You're stuck. Some of our kids' friends had undiagnosed learning disabilities, addicted parents, or had suffered traumas but never had resources or counseling to address these wounds. We saw kids drop out of high school, sell drugs, or end up dead or in jail.

These weren't faceless statistics, but neighbors.

Over time, our kids realized that our cash-poor family was actually privileged. Though they lacked the ski trips and sleek Suburbans of their cousins, they led cushy lives compared to many neighbors. Two parents hovered over them. Extended family stood ready if we needed a loan. Craig had learned budget-stretching home renovation skills from his father. We had social capital: connections who gave our kids their first summer jobs or wrote them reference letters.

Our kids saw the joy of generosity. For a number of years, our relatively low-income church had one of the highest per-capita giving ratios in our presbytery. Statistically, the poor are more generous than the middle class or wealthy. Proximity to need led many of Faith's attendees to be generous, both in their offerings and to individuals. "Someone" helped an immigrant buy a car. "Someone" loaned J. money to fix his truck. "Someone" paid for T.'s high school graduation gown.

Firsthand experience of different races and backgrounds shaped our children's careers. One daughter is an ER nurse in an urban hospital serving both privileged and impoverished residents. Another worked her way through graduate school in an upscale restaurant, equally comfortable with patrons and minimum-wage kitchen staff. Now, as a special education teacher, she works with kids and parents from many backgrounds. Our friendship with a Colombian family serving the poor in Bolivia sparked interest in Latin America for our third daughter, who eventually earned a Ph.D. in Latin American history. Our son attended several youth groups in high school, learning to build bridges between races and classes—an asset in the business world he now inhabits. Our youngest daughter is pursuing a master's degree in social work to become a child protection worker. They all have expressed gratitude for their cross-cultural background.

Our kids had front-row seats to today's most pressing issues: racial unrest, poverty, inequality, family breakdown, loss of jobs. They learned that there are no easy answers.

They recognized that while some people are born into good seats at society's banquet, others clear the tables or scrounge through the trashcans to survive. They felt in their bones that the playing field was not even. They saw our church model a response based in biblical justice: What would Jesus have us do?

> The first century world found the diversity of the early church compelling, and the gospel spread rapidly.

We did many things wrong as parents. Some of our kids found their teen years especially rocky as they tried to fit in somewhere, anywhere. I have discussed this in my first book, *A Thousand Resurrections*. But would living in a homogeneous suburb have changed that? There's no guarantee.

Perhaps, as our kids saw Jesus unite people from "every tribe and language and people and nation" (Rev. 5:9), they caught a vision for biblical unity. Perhaps they saw people serving one another. Perhaps they saw God's plan for bringing his shalom, his wholeness and peace, to a sin-damaged society.

The Benefits of Diverse Churches

For decades, business and education leaders have recognized the importance of including and interacting appropriately with people from other cultures. Sadly, the church often lagged behind. But this is changing. Many leaders want to know how to reach the varied people groups in their communities. Nurturing a more diverse church can be challenging. We might not know how or where to start.

The unity of believers across background, race, ethnicity, or other status is important not because it's politically correct, or even because of demographic realities, but because it is biblical. Churches should strive to reach all members of the community. When we fail to create an environment that welcomes different racial, ethnic, cultural, and economic groups, we forgo many blessings. One writer summarizes this, "Diversity is not a negative but a positive, not a curse but a blessing, not a threat but an opportunity."[1] Diverse churches benefit the body of Christ in a number of ways.

1. **Belonging to a diverse church can teach us how to relate in our multiethnic world.** Do we feel awkward or uncomfortable around people who are different from us? Could you feel comfortable talking to a Middle Eastern immigrant, a hip urban teen, an elderly Asian woman, a handicapped White man? Experience is an excellent teacher, and we usually learn more from our failures than our successes.

2. **We learn from the unique strengths of other communities.** Just as we are enriched by foods from other cultures, other worship styles and practices can be stimulating and thought-provoking. Is there only one "right" way to pray? Is it standing, kneeling, sitting, or laying prostrate on the floor? Do we take turns praying or all pray simultaneously out loud?
3. **Those who are suffering, fleeing persecution, or refugees can teach us how to endure with dignity and grace.** Theologian Thabiti Anyabwile says that in our post-Christian world, evangelicals can "learn to be the moral minority from a much older moral minority,"[2] the African American church. As persecution or suffering strip us of every support but God, we can learn from the example of others how to depend on him more fully.
4. **Diverse churches help us evaluate our own culture under the lens of Scripture.** John Stott writes, "Every culture, being a human construct, is a mixture of good and evil, truth and error, beauty and ugliness." He points out that after being carried into captivity in a foreign land, the prophet Daniel and his friends "resolved to assimilate all that was good in Chaldean culture but were equally determined to reject everything that was incompatible with their revealed faith."[3]
5. **The diversity of a community can expose my cultural sin.** As we view our own culture through others' eyes, we gain new insights. It pours Miracle-Gro on the sanctification process as I am stretched beyond my comfort zone. Can I tolerate discomfort? Do I expect the church to reflect my preferences at the expense of others' preferences? Am I reflecting Kingdom

values or my own? My impatience, my pride, my time pressures, my need to be right, my desire to be understood become clearer in a multicultural context.

6. **Diverse churches may be more welcoming to those who don't feel like they fit in at a traditional or monoethnic church.** In 2018-19, a Pew Research study found that 26% of Americans list their church affiliation as atheist, agnostic, or "nothing in particular."[4] Could these "nones and dones" find the multiethnic church's unity across multiple divides attractional? If my church is full of people from different segments of society, would my suit-wearing coworker and my denim-clad, super-tattooed neighbor both feel comfortable there? Would the recovering addict, the people on both ends of the political spectrum, or the returning citizen fit in? Is my church diverse enough that they wouldn't stand out? Who feels comfortable at my church?

Jesus said that the unity of his followers would demonstrate his messiahship and God's love (John 17) for all humanity. The first-century world found the diversity of the early church compelling, and as a result, the gospel spread rapidly.

HISTORY WINDOW 9

Native Americans, Part II

Manifest Destiny held that God had given America the land from the Atlantic to the Pacific. Never mind that First Nations peoples already occupied it. Westward and southward expansion led to coercive and broken treaties, forced removal, wars, and genocide. The "Indian Wars" that had started in the colonial period persisted until the 1890 Wounded Knee Massacre.

Citizenship seemed to offer Native Americans little protection. Even though the Cherokee had been recognized as U.S. citizens since 1817, President Andrew Jackson ordered their expulsion in the brutal Trail of Tears (1830-50). Chief Justice Roger Taney further extended citizenship to all Native Americans in 1857 (although Taney had withheld this right from African Americans a year earlier in the Dred Scott Decision). Still, the purging of Natives from desirable land continued.

The government broke treaties often, especially when gold was involved. After violating an 1851 agreement, the U.S. hammered out another treaty that granted the Sioux the Black Hills, a land they considered sacred. But when gold was discovered, settlers overran the area, and the government confiscated the land. Further south and west, during the

California Gold Rush, tens of thousands of Native Americans were killed, sometimes aided by state government, in the California Genocide (1849-1870).

Tens of thousands of Native American children were forcibly removed from their homes and sent to boarding schools to "kill the Indian and save the man."[16] At these schools, run by missionaries or the government, youth were stripped of their culture and language, punished harshly, and often subjected to abuse. As late as 1928, children at federal boarding schools were malnourished, overworked, and poorly educated.[17] The last residential school closed in 1973.[18]

Despite such ill treatment, Native Americans served in the U.S. military with distinction. General Ely Parker, a Seneca, served as Gen. U. S. Grant's secretary when Lee surrendered at Appomattox in 1865. Native Americans served in both World Wars, including the Navajo Code Talkers, whose encryption defied Japanese codebreakers in World War II.

The American Indian Movement (AIM), founded in 1968, advocated for much- needed reform and policy change. In 2009, President Obama signed a historic apology for past "ill-conceived policies by the U.S. government."[19]

Chapter 10

Race, Redemption, and the Multiethnic Church

One evening in June, 1963, when Carol was eight years old, her parents took her and her brothers to a Baltimore amusement park. She scurried onto the tilt-o-whirl. When the ride stopped, the police were waiting. Police lights flashed against the dark trees as officers interrogated her parents. "Who are you? Where do you come from?" Her father explained that they had lived in Baltimore all their lives. The family had German roots. His explanations didn't help. Carol and her family were forced to leave the park. They never returned.

Carol now knows they were ejected because of her race. Although the rest of her family is White, Carol is biracial; at this time, African Americans were not allowed in Gwynn Oak Park.

What was life like for Carol—born in 1955—in segregated Baltimore? While cherished at home, she encountered racism in her working-class, White neighborhood. She had kinky hair and olive skin; her brothers were pale and straight-haired. African Americans could not sit at lunch counters, try on clothes in department stores, or swim in Whites-only pools. Imagine the cruelty of children unleashed on a self-conscious, tall, biracial child in an all-White classroom. Or imagine a family outing: "These are our sons, Fred and Bill. And our daughter, Carol." Stunned silence. Awkward glances. Forced smiles. Once, a relative snapped, "We never had any Black in our family until you came along."

In the mid-1970s, as a new believer, Carol joined a multiethnic college ministry, and had Black, White, and Asian friends. But on Sunday mornings, the racial mixing ended. She had to choose between a White church and a Black one. For years, she was the only non-White member of her church.

When we started an intentionally multiethnic church in 1981, we heard mixed responses. "This is a nice experiment you've got here," one visitor remarked. "I predict doom," a seminary friend said. Others told us about churches that had split along racial lines. The homogeneous unit principle, embraced by seminaries and denominations at the time, argued that churches grow faster if people do not have to cross racial or ethnic lines. Birds of a feather flock together—and so do Jesus's sheep. But we believed our theological practice should be based not on expediency, or our preferences, but on the pages of Scripture. God made this dream a reality despite our youth, ignorance, and lack of experience.

In 2001, in *Divided by Faith*, sociologists Michael Emerson and Christian Smith found that "White evangelicalism likely does more to perpetuate racialized society than to reduce it."[1] This is not surprising; the Black church formed as a response to racism, and even during the Civil Rights era, some White churches turned away non-White worshippers. In 2001, only 10% of American congregations were multiethnic (with less than 80% of attendees from the same race or ethnicity). By 2019, 16% of all congregations were multiethnic.[2]

In 1996, Carol began attending our church. "There were people who were like me—biracial kids, interracial couples, Black and White. I feel like I fit in. Faith is a glimpse of what God wants us to be." Carol's sensitivity to being an outsider led her to serve as an usher and greeter and to befriend international students. "A multiethnic church is not without problems, but I see people trying very hard to work out their differences," she says. Carol still worships at Faith today.

Carol believes Jesus reconciles us not only to God, but to each other as spiritual brothers and sisters. She remembers the words of Dr. Martin Luther King Jr. "The end is reconciliation; the end is redemption; the end is the creation of the beloved community."[3]

Are We Reaching Our Diverse Neighbors?

America has undergone a profound demographic shift. In California, Florida, Texas, and a few other states, Whites are already one minority among other minorities. In many neighborhoods, we have the opportunity to meet people from around the world.

- In 2018, one in four U.S. residents was an immigrant or the child of an immigrant.[4]
- Babies of color are now in the majority.[5]
- From 2000-2010, the Asian American population increased by 43%.[6]
- Today, Chinese Americans are our largest Asian population at 2.5 million.[7]
- By 2045, Whites will no longer be in the majority in the U.S.[8]
- By 2050, one in three residents will be Hispanic.[9]
- Generation Z, those born after 1998, is the most ethnically diverse generation in U.S. history.[10]

How is the church faring in reaching our diverse neighbors? While the concept of a multiethnic church may appeal to many people, most aren't willing to adjust to make this happen.

- Two-thirds of American churchgoers (67%) say their church has done enough to become racially diverse. Less than half think their church should become more diverse.[11]
- Evangelicals (71%) are most likely to say their church is diverse enough, and Whites (37%) are least likely to say their church should become more diverse.[12]

Although the percentage of multiethnic churches has increased, a deeper study by Dr. Korie Edwards reveals that "they are not delivering on what they promised. "Multiethnic churches often celebrate being diverse for diversity's sake … people of color in multiracial churches are often relegated to roles that are more symbolic ... but that have no real influence or authority in the church."[13]

People of color face challenges in a majority-culture space and often feel marginalized because White cultural preferences dominate. "Multiracial churches tend to mimic white churches in their culture and theology ... [they] work—that is, remain diverse—to the extent that their white members are comfortable."[14]

After the divisive 2016 election, the percentage of Blacks in multiracial churches dropped. The multiple killings of unarmed Black men, the 2020 election, the Capitol riot, the rise in anti-Asian sentiment, and the White church's silence on many of these issues led to a further exodus of prominent Black evangelicals from multiethnic churches or majority-White congregations.[15] What one newspaper chronicled as a "quiet exodus" became for some a call to "Leave Loud."[16]

Why are we so divided when our theology so clearly explains that we are united in Christ? As Paul pens his letter to the Galatians, his passion leaps off the page: he is "astonished" that believers in Galatia are abandoning the gospel. He says—twice—"But even if we or an angel from heaven should preach a gospel other than the one we preached to you, let them be under God's curse!" (Gal. 1:8) What is this aberrant gospel? Justification by works, not faith in Christ. In this case, that meant justification through their ethnic group—birth into Abraham's extended family—or by following the Jewish law.

Paul rejects these options, insisting that we are saved by faith in Jesus alone. Groups that were culturally and socially at odds are now united in Christ. "There is neither Jew nor Gentile, neither slave nor free, there is no male and female, for you are all one in Christ Jesus. If you belong to Christ, then you are Abraham's seed, and heirs according to the promise" (Gal. 3:28-29). He returns to this theme again in Ephesians, expounding on the "mystery" that Jews and Gentiles are united in Christ. "Through the gospel the Gentiles are heirs together with Israel, members together of one body, and sharers together in the promise in Christ Jesus" (Eph. 3:6).

The multiethnic church is difficult. White worshippers may struggle to adjust worship styles, music, etc. to accommodate other cultural expressions. People may believe their cultural preferences are a biblical imperative. Wise leaders of multiethnic churches help people understand that in blending cultural expressions, their personal preferences may not be met. They share a "10% or 20% rule": people should expect to be uncomfortable at least 10% of the time. One's personal worship preferences (type of music, song/hymn selections) will only be expressed 80-90% of the time.

Starting a multiethnic church, or diversifying an existing church, takes clear intention, biblical teaching, and wise implementation. Are worshippers willing to

> Starting a multiethnic church, or diversifying an existing church, takes clear intention, Biblical teaching, and wise implementation.

adjust their preferences to welcome neighbors from other backgrounds? To adjust worship or music styles? Multiethnic churches offer opportunities for members to hear, know, and love one another to preserve "the unity of the Spirit through the bond of peace" (Eph. 4:3).

HISTORY WINDOW 10

The "Yellow Peril": Anti-Asian Sentiment in America

An influx of Chinese immigrants in the 1850's added to the nation's diversity. Many Chinese peasants, impoverished because of natural disasters and the Opium Wars with Great Britain, immigrated during the California Gold Rush (1848) and played a pivotal role building the Transcontinental Railroad. When violence broke out against them, they could not seek justice; an 1854 Supreme Court case ruled that the Chinese, like African Americans and Native Americans, could not testify in court.

During the nineteenth-century, the metaphor of East Asians as a "yellow peril" dangerous to Western civilization emerged. Residents of China, Japan, and other Eastern nations were depicted as unclean, uncivilized, or dangerous. When economic depression and unemployment increased hostility to Chinese American workers, Congress passed its first ethnic-specific anti-immigration law: the Chinese Exclusion Act (1882). It was not until 1943 that all restrictions on Chinese immigration were lifted.

While the U.S. had allowed citizens of African ancestry to become naturalized citizens after the Civil War, citizenship was not extended to other non-White groups until many decades later. As late as 1922, the Supreme Court ruled that Asian

Americans could not become naturalized citizens. Other "undesirable" immigrants were targeted in the Immigration Act of 1924. Finally, in 1952, the U.S. ended a race-based system for citizenship.[20]

Perhaps America's most infamous anti-Asian event occurred after the U.S. declared war with Japan. In 1942, President Franklin D. Roosevelt signed Executive Order 9066, ordering all people of Japanese descent interred in isolated, hastily constructed, crude camps. Some 120,000 Japanese Americans lost their homes and businesses. While some denominations and individual Christians ministered to the needs of camp internees, the American church was largely caught up in anti-immigrant hysteria. In 1988, President Reagan signed the Civil Liberties Act, which offered an official apology and modest reparations.

After World War II, Asians began to be viewed as the "model minority" because of their economic success. However, Anti-Asian sentiment was only dormant, not defeated; it flared during the 2003 SARS epidemic and again during COVID-19, which some labeled the "Chinese virus." Even today, Asian American white-collar professionals are less likely than any other race to be promoted into management roles. White professionals are twice as likely to be promoted to such management roles.[21]

Chapter 11

The Miseducation of Maria Garriott

In college, I landed my dream summer job as a park ranger at Fort Sumter National Monument in Charleston, where South Carolina militiamen fired the first shots of the Civil War in 1861. I lived with the other summer workers nearby, in a former Coast Guard station on Sullivan's Island. After work, we'd sit on the wide nineteenth-century porch to smell the sea breeze and admire the lighthouse in our backyard.

Two summers as a park ranger sparked my enduring interest in Civil War history. My job orientation included facts about the war, Charleston, and the fort. I learned of fiery politicians, colorful dandies, female spies, and steadfast generals.

But I never learned about the Black bodies.

Two decades after my idyllic summer, I learned that nearly half of the enslaved Africans arriving in America's British colonies between 1700 and 1775 had passed through Charleston. They disembarked from their horrific voyage to quarantine at a "pestilence house" on Sullivan's Island. The dead were buried in mass graves. Worse, some ship captains jettisoned their dead and dying cargo in the harbor.

Men, women, and children tossed overboard. Bloated bodies washed up on Sullivan's Island. The stench of death on my beach.

This gruesome detail and others about slavery in Charleston hadn't appeared in the books I'd been given to prepare me to interact with visitors. The omission felt like a betrayal.

Of course, I'd known of Charleston's role as a bastion of slavery. Tourism brochures mentioned that downtown, amid the grand houses, a plaque marked the former slave market. But details of what the South called its "peculiar institution" were obliquely alluded to or absent altogether. No bloodied backs, no raped women, no children torn from mother's arms. No coffles of chained men and women marched hundreds of miles to farm cotton in the southwest. Charleston wished to be known for genteel plantations and hoop skirts rather than the auction block and the lash.

Even as a book-loving, college-educated adult, I had massive gaps in my knowledge of American history. I didn't know that even after Congress banned the transatlantic slave trade, New York and Baltimore supported it through shipbuilding and finance. I didn't know that Nat Turner's rebellion was one of more than 250 slave revolts. I didn't know how sharecropping trapped the formerly enslaved in poverty for generations or that lynching claimed more than 4,400 men and women between 1877 and 1941. I didn't know about race riots like Wilmington, Tulsa, and Rosewood, in which hundreds of African American men and women were massacred. I didn't know that the New Deal was tailored to exclude Blacks. Except for a few tepid paragraphs, my education had largely erased the contributions and suffering of millions of enslaved Americans, the trauma they endured after Emancipation, and other aspects of our racial past. My education had failed me.

I certainly didn't know about American Christianity's complicity in racism: how Puritan luminaries like Jonathan Edwards and George Whitfield had owned slaves. The first Black denomination, the African Methodist Episcopal Church (AME) was founded in 1816 in response to racist exclusion. I knew the heroic narratives of Christian abolitionists, but not that their cause was widely dismissed for many decades. The Southern church created a theology to justify slavery.

The financial ramifications of slavery boggle the mind. In 1850, a decade before the Civil War, four million Americans were enslaved.[1] The debt would come due: four years of unrelenting civil war. And another century of pain and strife.

Ponder this: one group of people owned another. How would that feel? A friend said recently, "I have in-laws in the South who have told me that slaves actually had it better when they were slaves. I asked them, 'How would you feel if the farm had a bad year and I needed to sell your children to make my mortgage?'"

Learning about Sullivan's Island's role in slavery fueled my hunger to know more. The best antidote to ignorance is knowledge, so I've devoured books on America's racial history. I can't keep up; scholars unearth new findings daily from archives, libraries, and other sources. As I visit national parks, I see evidence that today's National Park Service intentionally shares histories and voices previously overlooked.

I wanted to see the past and the present more accurately, more honestly. As a nation and as a church, we are grappling with the lingering ramifications of our past. May we look to God for true healing and reconciliation. We cannot look away.

Examining How We Got Here

There is biblical precedent for examining our past. We celebrate God's work and miraculous interventions, lament our sin, and move forward in repentance and faith. "Remember" appears more than 200 times in the Bible, in passages such as Deut. 7:18: "You shall not be afraid of them but you shall remember what the Lord your God did to Pharaoh and to all Egypt." We are to tell his wonders to our children and to our children's children. Remembering our history provides courage and instruction, warnings and reminders.

To understand our nation today, we must unflinchingly examine our past. Current racial and economic disparities have historical roots. In *White Awake*, Pastor Daniel Hill contrasts two views of America's past. "White Americans remember a history of discovery, manifest destiny, opportunity, American exceptionalism. Communities of color, especially those with African and indigenous roots, remember a history of stolen lands, broken treaties, slavery, boarding schools, segregation, cultural genocide, internment camps, and mass incarceration."[2]

The ugly chapters of America's past and present are a manifestation of the Fall. The propensity to oppress those who are less powerful is part of our human sin nature, a sin problem not a skin problem. Obviously, one racial or ethnic group is not inherently more sinful than any other—Scripture disproves that notion, as does world history. Consider the Israelites under Pharaoh, the Holocaust, apartheid South Africa, the Armenian genocide of 1915-17, the post-Soviet Union Yugoslav war, Rwandan massacre, the Sri Lankan civil war, and recently, the persecution of Uighurs in China. Conflicts are a complicated mix of ethnic, political, social, religious, or economic factors.

> The propensity to oppress those who are less powerful is part of our human sin nature.

The deaths of George Floyd, Ahmaud Arbery, Breonna Taylor, and others shook America's illusion of being a post-racial, colorblind society. For minority communities already disproportionally affected by the coronavirus and the subsequent economic fallout, these deaths were yet another traumatic reminder that justice is, indeed, not doled out equally.

Pastor and author Randy Nabors points out that it is often hard for some people to understand how past events still resonate today for minorities. "Most in the majority and dominant White culture have little idea of what it is like to live as a minority in our nation. We neither understand the pain of being insulted, overlooked, and dismissed because of our physical appearance, nor do we appreciate the pain of history. We miss the relevance of historic racism and how it relates to immediate events of injustice against members of a minority group."

While many Christian organizations, denominations, and individuals spoke out in support of racial justice, others suggested the protests overstated America's racial inequalities. Some people dismissed the protests and pointed to the socialist/Marxist or anarchist objectives of a small minority of demonstrators.

Acknowledging past racial oppression does not necessarily mean people are willing to do anything about today's racial disparities. The 2020 protests led some American Christians to push back against the idea of addressing historical racial injustice. While a Barna poll of self-identified Christians found that 26% strongly agreed that historically the U.S. has oppressed minorities, the percentage of those who said they were not motivated to address racial injustice actually grew (from 17% in 2019 to 30% in 2020). Barna suggests that "those who might have previously been on the fence about addressing racial injustice have become more firmly opposed to engaging."[3]

Yet what do we, as followers of Jesus, do about our painful racial and ethnic divisions, even within the church? If the Bible preaches the beauty of God's diverse humanity and God's abhorrence of injustice (especially toward the poor, the orphan, or the stranger), how do we respond today?

HISTORY WINDOW 11

Latinx America, Part 1

Hispanic and Latinos are our largest ethnic or racial minority (18.5% of the U.S. population).[22] Although the terms are often used interchangeably, "Hispanic" and "Latino/Latina/Latinx" can have slightly different connotations. Hispanic refers to someone of Spanish or Spanish-speaking descent living in the U.S., while Latinx refers to a person of Latin American origin or descent living in the United States. A Latinx or Hispanic person can be any race or color.

Hispanic/Latinx American history has often been neglected, especially when we consider that Spanish colonizers preceded other Europeans. One professor explains, "The ignorance of the Hispanic dimension of U.S. history is stunning. Until now, American history has been dominated by Anglo Saxon culture, a tradition that dates to scholarship of the nineteenth century when the British Empire reigned supreme."[23]

The Spanish Empire once stretched across the southwestern U.S. through Central and South America to the tip of Chile. Columbus initiated Spanish colonization of the Americas in 1492. Almost 100 years before Jamestown and Plymouth Rock, Spanish explorer Ponce de Leon hacked his way through Southern Florida (1513) in the first European exploration of the continent. America's oldest continually inhabited city is St. Augustine, Florida, established in 1565, which Spain ruled for more than 250 years. Santa Fe is the oldest American city west of the Mississippi (est. 1609) and was the first foreign capital captured by the U.S. (in 1846, during the Mexican-American War).[24] "The first explorers of the West were not Lewis and Clark; rather Coronado and Cabeza de Vaca were traversing the plains in the 1540s. Junipero Serra came north from Baja in the mid-1700s to establish monasteries along the California coast from San Diego to Monterrey".[25]

Spanish colonists fought the British in the American Revolution. "There were more Spaniards fighting in the U.S. Revolution than Americans. The Spanish gave more money than the French to support the American Revolution".[26]

Chapter 12

Social Justice? Biblical Justice?
Education for All

I plopped down on the rug in the church basement, inviting the children to sit around me. "It's time for our Bible story," I began.

Four-year-old Claire leaned forward across the semicircle and scanned the upside down teacher's guide in my lap. "Oh, you're going to tell us about Zacchaeus climbing the tree to see Jesus!" she crowed.

Claire, the child of a doctor and an engineer, was smart—even precocious. But a fluent reader upside down? Impressive.

Claire's reading ability underscored the inequalities at church. While some children found Sunday School curriculum too familiar or too easy, others struggled to read at all. Sometimes, even when they'd been asked in advance to read a Scripture passage during a service, teenagers flailed away at the text with wild guesses, unable to decode words. It was excruciating for both the reader and the congregation.

Stronger Together

In the 1980s and 1990s, Baltimore city's public school system was floundering. Compared to their suburban counterparts, city schools had a higher percentage of inexperienced teachers, children in poverty, children who had experienced trauma in their neighborhoods and families, and students with special needs. Some schools lacked basic resources—individual copies of textbooks, copy paper for teachers—and enrichment classes such as music or art. By the end of third grade, over half of students in low-income, minority neighborhoods were one to three years behind grade level in reading. This doomed them to a cycle of shame, special-ed classes, and discouragement. No wonder more than half of Baltimore students were dropping out before graduation, and a quarter of the adult population was functionally illiterate. Baltimore's cheery motto—"The City That Reads"—was more aspirational than actual. Lack of a diploma often led to unemployment, low wage jobs, or worst of all, the "underground economy"--crime.

Academic researchers at Johns Hopkins University labeled many of our neighborhood schools "dropout factories," asking, "If two 747s took off from Baltimore's airport every day loaded with children and crashed, wouldn't people do something about it?" Dr. Doug Mac Iver, one of these researchers, attended Faith and moved into the neighborhood. He saw in Baltimore's public schools "an educational famine of biblical proportions."

As I watched neighborhood kids flounder, and struggled to educate our children in this setting, I simmered with anger. These complicated problems were generational, societal, intractable. How could the schools be failing so many kids year after year?

Our church started an after-school tutoring program and summer camp to help students build the academic skills they needed, but these efforts felt like filling a bathtub one cup at a time. We considered partnering with our neighborhood schools, but realized deeper intervention was required. But how could our small church start a school? Raise sufficient funds? Find qualified teachers? Recruit students?

So in 1993, a team of people at Faith started Baltimore Christian School (BCS) based on the conviction that all children should have access to an excellent Christian education regardless of financial status. BCS based tuition on a sliding scale. We formed a nonprofit board, initially led by Dr. Mac Iver, that included church and neighborhood parents. We recruited dedicated teachers and enlisted volunteer tutors to help children reach or stay on grade level. We started with kindergarten and added a grade every year, all the way to 5th grade.

Children thrived in small classes with individual instruction. How proud we were when one year, the 5th grade debate team won the citywide competition among their peers, and beat the middle school debaters as well.

The school required significant leadership attention and money from the church. How do you pay staff decent salaries when students contribute only a fraction of the actual cost of their education? We hired development directors, solicited donors, applied for grants, and held fundraising events. Board members grew weary. Some staff moved on to other jobs. Then came the economic downturn of 2009. Increasingly dire requests yielded some donations—but not enough. After 18 years of operation, the board decided it needed to close the school.

The dream died hard for all of us—parents, teachers, and donors. We comforted ourselves that by that time, some schools had improved and several charter schools had emerged, offering parents more alternatives. BCS had provided hundreds of children with an academic foundation, character development and spiritual training. Some graduates went on to attend the city's best public or private schools. For a generation of students, God's people had provided educational justice so that children of single mothers, low-wage workers, and even some professionals could have the educational foundation they needed.

A Deeper Dive: Biblical Justice

How do we think biblically about social justice? Does "social justice" flow from a secular humanistic worldview or a biblical one? What does "social justice" mean and how do we achieve it?

Some Christians push back against the term "social justice." One writer suggests, "Our ecclesial-historical amnesia is so acute, our Old Testament literacy so anemic, and our cultural intelligence so low, that we associate social justice with Karl Marx rather than the Prophet Isaiah."[1]

While the term "social justice" is sometimes co-opted by Marxists, we should not dismiss it. Dr. Kelly Hamren, a professor at Liberty University, writes,

> What some are referring to as 'social justice' these days—making sure our laws and institutions don't make it easier for the powerful to oppress marginalized groups—often

> refers to good, old-fashioned biblical justice. ... Rejecting the concept outright robs Christians of the chance to become part of the conversation regarding its definition and application. ... Using the term in a way that validates biblical principles of justice can help shape the way in which the cultural conversation develops.[2]

Scripture tells us to be transformed by the renewing of our minds (Rom. 12:2). This renewal requires that we evaluate current worldviews in the light of God's Word. While our prevailing worldview (secular humanism) rejects the idea of a divine Creator and exalts human reason, a biblical worldview places the Judeo-Christian God at the center. While humanism believes that "man is the measure of all things," Christ-followers believe that "God is the measure of all things." Thus, we evaluate calls for social justice in light of God's revelation in Jesus and Scripture.

Even though "social justice" is espoused by a secular world, we recognize its roots in God's revelation. "All truth is God's truth" summarizes a statement from St. Augustine (AD 354-430): "Let every good and true Christian understand that wherever truth may be found, it belongs to his Master." John Calvin reiterated this idea during the Reformation: "All truth is from God; and consequently, if wicked men have said anything that is true and just, we ought not to reject it; for it has come from God."[3]

Even if a concept is phrased in biblical language, we should examine it to see if it harmonizes with all of God's revelation. Bible verses can be taken out of context to "prove" heresies, such as the "curse of Ham" (Gen. 9), which was used to support slavery. Satan himself quoted Scripture when he tempted Jesus in the wilderness

(Matt. 4). (While preaching on this passage, a pastor friend quipped, "Satan can pass an ordination exam.")

Social justice is a core value in biblical revelation. God's concern for the powerless and vulnerable in society flows throughout the Old and New Testament. Over and over, God calls his people to demonstrate justice: "He has told you, O man, what is good; and what does the LORD require of you but to do justice, and to love kindness, and to walk humbly with your God?" (Mic. 6:8). Just behavior is equated with and a hallmark of true righteousness, as opposed to a false piety or pretense.

> Social justice is a core biblical value. God's concern for the powerless and vulnerable flows throughout the Old and New Testament.

In ancient Israel, much like today, the most vulnerable community members were the poor, the orphan, the widow, and the immigrant. They lacked political power, social capital, or family connections to improve their lot. God established standards to protect them. He demanded that the sojourner (immigrant) and the fatherless be treated justly and widows be protected (Deut. 24:17). Israel was to have the same laws for the foreigner as the native born (Lev. 24:22). When harvesting, landowners were instructed to leave some crops on the margins for the poor to gather. These laws of gleaning dignified the poor by enabling them to provide for themselves (Lev. 19:9, 23:22).

Justice is a robust pursuit, full of active verbs: speak, correct, seek, plead, rescue. The mouth of the righteous person "speaks justice" (Ps. 37:30). God's people are to speak out for those who can't advocate for themselves (Prov. 31:8-9), including the unborn (Ps. 139:13-16). God condemned child sacrifice and infanticide (Ps. 106:36-38) and instituted penalties for causing a woman to miscarry (Exod. 21:23-24). We are to "rescue those who are being taken away to death; hold back those who are stumbling to the slaughter" (Prov. 24:11). We are not only to refrain from oppressive or unrighteous behavior, but to correct it: "seek justice, correct oppression; bring justice to the fatherless, plead the widow's cause" (Isa. 1:17).

God demands righteous business practices; he abhors partiality and bribes (Deut. 16:19), unequal scales and unequal measures (Amos 6:5-6; Prov. 20:10).

God promises to punish injustice. He destroyed Sodom and Gomorrah not just because of their sexual sin, but because of their overall unrighteousness. "Behold, this was the guilt of your sister Sodom: she and her daughters had pride, excess of food, and prosperous ease, but did not aid the poor and needy" (Ezek. 16:49). We should heed these words.

Jesus demonstrated true justice in word and deed. The prophet Isaiah had predicted that the coming Messiah would reign eternally "with justice and with righteousness" (Isa. 9:7). Jesus quoted from Isaiah's prophecy (Isa. 61:1-2) in his first sermon (Luke 4:17-19), proclaiming himself as its fulfillment. He condemned the Pharisees for neglecting justice, even though they scrupulously observed religious ritual. "Woe to you, scribes and

Pharisees, hypocrites! For you tithe mint and dill and cumin and have neglected the weightier matters of the law: justice and mercy and faithfulness. These you ought to have done, without neglecting the others." (Matt. 23:23; Luke 11:42).

Preferential treatment of the wealthy violates God's standards. When the early church struggled with the sin of partiality, the Apostle James swiftly corrected the believers. This behavior flowed from "evil thoughts" and was a sin against God (James 2:1-9).

While Christians can disagree on how to implement just policies, we must honor God's concern for righteous principles. The Lord promises a blessing for obedience to his commands of justice. "Blessed is the one who considers the poor! In the day of trouble the LORD delivers him; the Lord protects him and keeps him alive; he is called blessed in the land" (Ps. 41:1-2; Ps. 106:3). Our righteousness is a beacon, our "justice as the noonday" (Ps. 37:6).

HISTORY WINDOW 12

Latinx America, Part 2

Many parts of what is now the U.S. originally belonged to Mexico, which Spain had conquered. In 1845, The U.S. annexed Texas. A few years later, U.S. victory in the Mexican-American War (1846-48) set the border at the Rio Grande River and gave America half of Mexico's land: present-day California, New Mexico, Nevada, Utah, most of Colorado and Arizona, and part of present-day Oklahoma, Wyoming, and Kansas. The 100,000 Hispanics living in these territories became American citizens but often faced overt discrimination and racially-motivated crime, including lynching.

In spite of deep discrimination and race riots, the Mexican American population expanded from 5 million to 15 million between 1910-1930, as residents fled the Mexican Revolution. Unfortunately, "Mexican Americans were wanted for their sweat, their military service, their taxes, but not for their children or their company. ... Brown Americans were pushed into segregated communities, forbidden from serving on juries, their children made to attend 'Mexican' schools."[27] When the Great Depression hit, the U.S. began deporting Mexican immigrants.[28]

Half a million Mexican Americans served in World War II. To make up for war-related labor shortages, especially in agriculture, the U.S. created the Bracero Program, which allowed short-term Mexican workers into the U.S. Over the next several decades, millions of Mexicans and Central Americans entered the U.S. In the late 1960s, poor working conditions led Cesar Chavez of the National Farm Workers Association to advocate for farmworkers. They spearheaded a boycott of grapes and a five-year strike for the right of collective bargaining.[29]

Today, Latinos in the U.S are a diverse, complex group and an important part of our Christian community. They come from more than twenty Latin American countries, "each of which has its own unique historical relationship to European colonization, the trans-Atlantic slave trade and American immigration policies."[30] According to a 2016 study, most Hispanic Americans are Christian (76%); about 25% are Protestant. Fully half of all American Catholics are Hispanic.[31] Researchers estimate that by 2030, because of immigrant conversions and the growth of Protestantism in their home countries, half of all Latinos in the U.S. will identify as Protestant.[32]

Chapter 13

Repenting and Lamenting

Turning Away and Turning Toward

Like many in our independent culture, I initially resisted taking responsibility for America's racial sins. During the twenty-three years we lived in a hard-pressed, minority neighborhood, I often felt overwhelmed with the challenges of raising our family there. When my neighbor, a community activist, talked about "the Man" and the "System" I'd think, "I'm not the problem! I pay extra taxes and car insurance to live here! Our schools are failing! People break into my house! They steal my kids' bikes!" But whether I wanted to or not, my Whiteness represented "the Man."

I've heard similar pushback from others. "I'm not racist. I've never joined a White supremacy organization. I never burned a cross on anyone's lawn. My family never owned slaves. Why am I responsible?" Others say, "Conversations about racial justice leave me feeling guilty for being White."

Americans tend to reject the concept of collective responsibility. Why should I repent of the sins of my nation? Is collective responsibility biblical? Do I bear any responsibility for America's racial sins?

The Bible presents a connected humanity, especially within the family of believers. God establishes a relationship with his people, first through Adam, then through Abraham and David. All became tainted by sin through Adam, and all who believe in Jesus receive his sinless record. While we are individually responsible for our actions, we also bear collective responsibility.

The prophet Nehemiah offers the best example of taking collective responsibility for sin, repenting, lamenting, and moving forward. He asks God to forgive the sins of his ancestors and grieves the consequences of this sin. Only after a season of lament does he act.

While all sin is ultimately against God, it frequently involves wrongdoing against another person. In Psalm 51:4, after his adultery with Bathsheba, David laments, "Against you, you only have I sinned and done what is evil in your sight." But he had also sinned against Bathsheba and her husband, Uriah. David laments the root of his sin: his rebellion against God.

Repentance requires changing direction. It's not just a verbal affirmation but adjusting or transforming our behavior. Repentance owns the impact of its actions and turns toward the person wronged. Rather than saying, "Can't you just get over it?" it asks, "How have I hurt you?" Repentance listens rather than defending, explaining, or justifying. It doesn't offer excuses.

Despite the discomfort, the truly repentant person enters into the other's suffering.

My ancestors didn't enslave people (as far as I know). But history and sociological research prove that I benefit from past and current structures that have favored one group of people over others. Theologically, I accept that I am not aware of all my transgressions—which include sins of racial partiality. I don't need to deny responsibility, be paralyzed by guilt, or descend into the self-destructive spiral of shame. I can respond with courage, rather than callous indifference. Like Nehemiah, I begin with acknowledging the sins of my ancestors and my nation, and lamenting. I turn from that and turn toward my brothers and sisters of color to lament with them.

The Importance of Lament

In 1961, writer James Baldwin condemned the "extraordinary and criminal indifference ... of most white people in this country" and their ignorance of the historic and current injustices African Americans faced. He said, "To be a Negro in this country and to be relatively conscious is to be in a rage almost all the time."[1] In 2017, after realizing his own racial privilege and cultural blindness, Pastor Daniel Hill wrote a corollary to Baldwin's quote. "To be a white person in this country and to be relatively conscious is to be in a state of lament almost all the time. To be awake is to see clearly the sorrows that come in this world."[2]

The Bible is unflinchingly realistic about grief. Nearly half of the psalms are laments. Many are communal or corporate laments, such as Psalm 9. Lament helps us process pain and suffering and cry out to God. Rather than deny or repress, we face suffering and turn to the one who has the power to help or sustain us. Grieving before God—like true repentance—brings healing.

> Grieving before God—like true repentance—brings healing.

When we grasp the historic and current ramifications of our national racial sins, like Nehemiah we must first lament. Otherwise, we may move too quickly to fixing to avoid feeling discomfort, guilt, or shame. Lament is an important precursor to tangible deeds of justice.

The Western evangelical church often avoids corporate responsibility for sin and lament. Theologian Dr. Soong-Chan Rah says, "We are too busy patting ourselves on the back over the problem-solving abilities of the triumphant American church to cry out to God in lament."[3]

A recent Barna poll asked how the church should respond to America's 400-year history of injustice against African Americans. One-third of White practicing Christians felt there was nothing the church could do (while only 15% of Black Americans felt this way). Overall, 26% of responders said they didn't know how the church should respond. Millennials were most likely to say the church should repent and work to repair the damage.

Rather than evading America's history of race-based sin, we must face it. Learning about our past, listening to the experiences of people of color, and lamenting empathetically are the first steps in racial reconciliation. Rather than denying or self-justifying, we engage humbly.

Black Lives Matter as an Expression of Lament

The Black Lives Matter (BLM) movement is a secular lament for the fact that Black lives have often not been treated equally in America. The movement formed as a response to the deaths of several unarmed Black men including Trayvon Martin (Florida, 2012), Eric Garner (New York, 2014), Michael Brown, (Ferguson, Missouri, 2014), and Freddie Gray (Baltimore, 2015). The deaths of Breonna Taylor (Kentucky, 2020), Tamir Rice (Ohio, 2020), and George Floyd (Minnesota, 2020) at the hands of police officers fueled additional protests.

Statistics on police-involved deaths in the U.S. indicate that Blacks, Latinos, and Native Americans are significantly more likely to be killed by police than White men.[4] In addition, racial disparities permeate the criminal justice system.

Nearly half of Black Americans say they have been unfairly stopped by police because of their race and ethnicity, while only 9% of White Americans say they've had this experience.[5] Even though most illegal drug users and dealers are White, three-fourths of those imprisoned for drug offenses have been Black or Latino.[6] People of color are incarcerated at disproportionally higher rates, with longer sentences. For example, the prison sentence for just 5 grams of crack cocaine (used more in urban communities) is the same as the sentence for 500 grams of powdered cocaine (favored by more privileged suburbanites). One in three Black males, and one in six Latino boys will go to prison at some point in their lives.[7] While economic disparities surely affect judicial outcomes—those who can afford to hire a lawyer versus who can't—the overwhelming evidence is that justice is not colorblind. Race matters.

As followers of Jesus, we must differentiate between the sentiment that Black lives matter and the Black Lives Matter organization. In a world that embraces sound bites over substantive discussion, many Christians find it hard to separate the movement from the message. The sentiment or slogan asks people to consider: Are killings of unarmed Black men isolated events or part of a systemic pattern of not valuing Black people? Of course all lives matter—but when viewed through the arc of history, even up to the present day, not all lives have mattered equally.

As an organization, however, BLM embraces some views antithetical to Christianity. The BLM movement is a broad, decentralized network advocating various structural and police reforms, some of which are nebulous or troubling. A statement that "We disrupt the Western-prescribed nuclear family structure requirement by supporting each other as extended families and 'villages' that collectively care for one another, especially our children, to the degree that mothers, parents, and children are comfortable" was removed from the website in 2020.[8] Its founders have been quoted as embracing Marxism, a diffuse school of thought that interprets class and social struggle through the lens of historical materialism.[9] Finally, the BLM call to "defund the police" is unnecessarily provocative and subject to wildly divergent interpretations.

However, the BLM movement has struck a deep nerve and called attention to injustices that persist today. Perhaps if Christians had more visibly and corporately pursued racial justice and reconciliation, then such a movement might not have been necessary or resonated so deeply. Perhaps if more Christians lived lives of radical generosity, fewer people would call for Marxist-style mandated redistribution. Rather than dismissing it outright, we should evaluate it under the lens of biblical truth.

HISTORY WINDOW 13

The Civil War and Reconstruction

When the festering boil of slavery erupted in the Civil War in 1861, Christian denominations that hadn't already split along sectional lines parted ways. Most Southern theologians such as Presbyterian Robert Dabney accepted slavery as God-ordained and promulgated the "curse of Ham" heresy that claimed God ordained Africans as a permanent servant class. Theologian James Thornwell advocated a "spirituality of the church" that declared that the church must remain silent on slavery and other "political" matters, deeming them a matter of personal conscience. This doctrine continues to influence the American church in key debates such as abortion, immigration, and other moral issues.

As the Civil War crystalized into a war to free the slaves as well as to preserve the Union, Lincoln recognized the strategic necessity of enlisting Black troops and allowed for their recruitment. These regiments, including the 54th Massachusetts, fought doggedly, even though Confederates executed or enslaved captured African American soldiers.

Finally, the 13th Amendment (passed just before Lincoln's assassination in 1865) outlawed involuntary servitude except for punishment of a crime. Unfortunately, this loophole would be used to justify convict labor in the Jim Crow era. The 14th and 15th Amendments granted all those born in the U.S. the right of citizenship, equal protection under the law, and the right to vote. During the early years after the Civil War, Black Americans started schools and businesses and held public office.

The new gains of Reconstruction would be short-lived. In 1877, to appease Southern Democrats after a disputed election, government troops withdrew from the South. Without the presence and protection of the federal government, the rights of Black Americans were crushed as new "Jim Crow" laws were passed.

Chapter 14

Privileges and Rights

Waking Up to White Privilege

When we lived in a working-class African American neighborhood called Pen Lucy, the area was so monoethnic that police stopped my teen daughters for "walking while White." ("Where are you going? Are you lost?") When I voted, officials waved me over to the table for the nearby, largely White district.

Once, as I spied an older White man walking down my street, I thought, "What's he doing here?" before recognizing him. At community meetings, my husband and I might be the only Caucasians, except for a visiting police officer or politician. I became acutely aware of my Whiteness.

Instead of being unaware of race, I now spent energy thinking about it. Instead of blending in, I stuck out. Instead of being evaluated on my individual behavior, I might be a stand-in for my whole race. I had the unusual experience— for a White person—of carrying the weight of my race.

Whether I wanted to or not, I represented 400 years of America's racial history. People who looked like me were the enslavers, lynchers, cross-burners, segregationists, and slumlords. People who looked like me had created the systems and structures that often excluded or stripped rights from Black, Latinx, Native, and Asian Americans. People who looked like me were often oblivious to the toll of racism on our brothers and sisters of color.

I found that every interaction or conflict could be imbued with racial overtones. If a woman in the neighborhood snubbed my greeting, was this because I was White or because she was having a bad day? Church conflicts were more complex because they were freighted with race—worship style preferences, conflict resolution styles, hiring decisions. A neighbor quoted early Malcolm X to my husband, calling him "a blue-eyed White devil man." One day, as a four-year-old neighbor helped plant marigolds in my yard, she confided, "White people be bad." Then she looked at me, shocked, and ran home. Even though I intentionally built cross-racial friendships, I could not escape the color of my skin.

When I first heard "White privilege" I pushed back. "I earned my grades. I worked hard at my jobs. What special benefits do I get for being White? I'm not feeling it in this neighborhood." I had only a superficial awareness of the persistent, pernicious effects of racialized policies embedded in our national history, laws that had promoted one group of people at the expense of another. Laws that had benefited me.

For example, White privilege paid for my college education. My WWII- veteran father finished college under the G.I. Bill and used low-interest VA loans to buy homes in good school districts.

The equity my parents accumulated helped fund college for their five children. But few African American veterans benefited from the G.I. Bill because segregated Southern universities refused to admit them.

Banks or mortgage agencies often turned away Black applicants or steered them into "contract buying" loans, where a single missed payment could trigger foreclosure.

Discriminatory housing covenants and redlining restricted minorities to less- desirable neighborhoods, creating overcrowded urban ghettos. Even in the 1980s— decades after the 1965 Fair Housing Act—my husband and I experienced the vestiges of the redlining that had created Baltimore's hyper-segregated neighborhoods. One bank told us it would approve our loan, but "not in that neighborhood."

White privilege meant that even though we lived in a lower-income community, my ten-year-old could ride his bike in a nearby wealthy, White enclave without arousing suspicion. But when he brought his Black friend, the neighborhood security guard stopped them. "We're just checking IDs today," the guard said.

White privilege protected my brother's economic future. When he got into trouble with drugs in college, my parents paid his bail and hired a lawyer who got the charges dropped. If convicted, he wouldn't have later had a successful thirty-five-year government career. I've known many young Black men who have been unfairly arrested and not had adequate legal representation or bail money.

Whiteness was codified and privileged from race-based laws in the 1700s, to the establishment of America's chattel slavery system, to the failure of post-Civil War Reconstruction, to Jim Crow laws, to the Depression-era New Deal and Fair Deal programs, to discriminatory post-WWII housing covenants, to mass incarceration in the War on Drugs. One scholar compared White privilege to "an invisible weightless knapsack of special provisions, maps, passports, codebooks … and blank checks."[1]

White privilege doesn't mean that Whites haven't worked hard or struggled. It doesn't mean that a poor White woman from Appalachia has the same amount of privilege as a middle-class woman in an affluent area. The concept acknowledges that brick by brick, over time, laws and policies piled one on top of another created an advantaged place for those deemed "White." Without any effort or desire on my part, these benefits flow to me. This is less a matter of individual racist actions than of entrenched advantages.

We shouldn't feel guilty for having absorbed the culture we've been saturated in all our lives. We shouldn't feel guilty for the ethnic or racial group God in his sovereignty ordained for us. But we should recognize and reject systems that have privileged some people or groups at the expense of others.

I still benefit from White privilege. I'm not afraid a routine traffic stop might end with my death. I tend to receive the benefit of the doubt; I won't get shot while jogging or peeking into a house under construction. I don't look "suspicious" in a hoodie. Women don't clutch their purses when I step into an elevator. Clerks in upscale department stores don't watch to see if I shoplift. I'm not asked to speak for or represent all the people in my racial or ethnic group. In places of power, I can be invisible; I blend in.

Before moving into an under-resourced minority neighborhood, it was easy for me to be blind to race-based injustices. I didn't experience them. That is part of the luxury of White privilege: I didn't have to think about race. But now, sensitized to historical record and present realities, I do.

Leveraging Privilege and Renouncing Rights

The Apostle Paul didn't deny his privilege but recognized it as part of God's sovereign plan to use him to spread the gospel. He leveraged his Jewish heritage, education, and Roman citizenship to serve Christ. He set aside some of his rights— such as his right to be financially supported as a respected rabbi—to spread the good news of Jesus. A true cross-cultural missionary, he crossed into the Gentile world, rather than demanding that others come into his.

> The Apostle Paul didn't deny his privilege, but recognized it as part of God's plan to spread the gospel.

As a Roman citizen, Paul was entitled to rights others lacked. After being beaten and imprisoned without a trial, Paul tells officials in Philippi that he and Silas are Roman citizens (Acts 16). Alarmed, the officials agree to escort the men safely out of the city. In Acts 22, the Roman commander prepares to have Paul flogged, but releases him upon learning he is a Roman citizen. Paul later uses his citizenship to appeal to be tried before Caesar (Acts 25), earning an audience for the faith before the most powerful man in the ancient world. In all these cases, Paul strategically leveraged his rights. He responded not from injured pride, but in a way to dignify the gospel and increase its hearing.

Where did Paul get the power to give up privileges and rights? From Jesus, who said, "Just as I have loved you, you also are to love one another. By this all people will know that you are my disciples, if you have love for one another" (John 13:34-35). Love is the driving power.

Privilege in itself isn't evil. But how do we use it? Do we keep it for ourselves or use it for the good of others and to gain a hearing for the gospel?

White Supremacy, White Fragility, and Mutual Responsibility

The term "White supremacy" is guaranteed to raise objections from some people. First, let's agree on a definition, look at our historical context, and then consider whether there is biblical support for this concept.

Merriam-Webster defines White supremacy as "the belief that the white race is inherently superior to other races and that white people should have control over people of other races." It is also "the social, economic, and political systems that collectively enable white people to maintain power over people of other races."[2]

As we have seen, racial or ethnic dominance is a human problem; people generally seek to maintain their political, economic, or social power, even if this is violent or oppressive. In the United States, this desire for power over others has manifested itself in the transatlantic slave trade, Jim Crow laws, and policies or laws that disadvantage minorities. Many Americans are unaware of the scope, pervasiveness, and persistence of these unjust laws or practices, and the "History Window" sections in this book seek to provide this information.

This global problem is because of sin, not skin. All humans, with the exception of Jesus the God-Man, are sinners (Rom. 3:23). Sociologist George Yancey writes, "People of all races can and do engage in sin, even the sin of racism. All major racial groups have exploited other groups when they had power."[3] People favor institutional systems that help their own group, even at the expense of other groups. "This pairs with the doctrine of human depravity; because we are all sinners, we tend to meet our own needs and the needs of those close to us."[4] White supremacy acknowledges the fact that in the U.S., Whites have historically had more power and thus have set up laws and policies that favored them.

Authors and pastors Duke Kwon and Gregory Thompson describe White supremacy as "a massive, multigenerational project of cultural theft" of identity, truth, power, and wealth.[5]

How do we create a more just, equitable society? Secular solutions emphasize education and human perfectibility, believing that "we can use reason to determine the best approach, and we can socialize others to accept it. This overconfidence has only furthered the ongoing racial conflict and fueled the cycle of racial hatred that plagues our society."[6]

Robin DiAngelo, author of *White Fragility*, believes that racism shouldn't be defined as behavior limited to extremists or "bad people"; individuals can often unconsciously perpetuate racism because of their implicit bias. She writes that American Whites—because they have largely been insulated from race-based stress—tend to respond with anger, guilt, fear, defensiveness, tears, or a refusal to engage when challenged about race. Some reviewers see flaws in her lack of empirical research and her solutions. "Her assumption that all people have a racist bias is reasonable—science has demonstrated it. The problem is what DiAngelo thinks must follow as the result of it."[6] Sociologist George Yancey writes, "White fragility is an academic way to tell white people to be quiet and listen ... [It] effectively silences dissenting voices."[7] Most significantly, it does not take human sin into account and naïvely assumes that people of color will not abuse their authority.

Instead, Yancey proposes a model rooted in biblical values. "The mutual responsibility model takes our sin nature into account and puts obligations on both majority and minority group members, because the sins of both ... contribute to racial tension."[8] "The sin nature is universal for people of all races, but how the sin nature manifests itself is clearly different for majority group members and for people of color."[9] Both Whites and people of color have mutual responsibilities in the task of racial healing. He suggests Christians focus on our common identity in Christ, engage in dialogue and active listening, work for win-win solutions, and confront racial problems with repentance and grace.

"Contrary to the questionable research surrounding white fragility, research suggests that a common identity and fruitful interracial contact can reduce prejudice.... The mutual accountability approach is more likely to produce unity across racial and ideological groups since it doesn't force anyone to ignore their own group interest—only to compromise a bit."[10] Then, perhaps we can fulfill the biblical mandate of Philippians 2:4, "Let each of you look not only to his own interests, but also to the interests of others."

HISTORY WINDOW 14

Jim Crow: Separate but Not Equal

The collapse of Reconstruction in 1877 solidified the power of Southern Democrats who wanted to regain political power and roll back Black gains. Newly passed "Jim Crow" laws disenfranchised and segregated Blacks, cementing the "separate but equal" doctrine in Southern life. Named after a blackface minstrel character that mocked Blacks, the term fails to capture the callousness of these laws, the scope of their reach, and the brutality with which they were enforced. Jim Crow laws suppressed Black votes—and thus, political voice or power—with poll taxes, literacy tests, land ownership requirements, and grandfather clauses. Sharecropping kept many formerly enslaved people destitute for generations, and the convict-lease system legally provided cheap labor for corporations and local governments. Blacks were relegated to separate (and usually inferior) schools, parks, prisons, hospitals, public transportation, public facilities, and colleges. Separate Bibles were used in some courtrooms.

To enforce White supremacy, vigilante groups emerged. The Ku Klux Klan "fused Christianity, nationalism, and White supremacy into a toxic ideology of hate,"[33] using intimidation, rape, arson, and lynching. The Klan was not a solely Southern phenomenon; fueled by anti-immigrant sentiment, its ranks swelled in the North and Midwest from 1910-1930. Lynching claimed the lives of more than 4,400 men and women between 1877 and 1941.[34] While most victims of this domestic terrorism were Southern Black men, Latinos, Native Americans, Asians, (and in at least one instance, 11 Italian Americans) were also lynched. In general, the most significant institution in America—the church—did little to address it. Black Americans organized to protect their rights, forming The National Association for the Advancement of Colored People (1909) and other organizations.

The Southern "Lost Cause" myth, which began shortly after the end of the Civil War and picked up steam in the late 1800s, enshrined the power of White society, painting the South as a victimized, idyllic Christian community invaded by the aggressive, godless North. Like a civil religion, the Lost Cause immortalized Confederate generals, lauded enslavers' role as humane "civilizers" of grateful Black people and rewrote the war as a conflict over "states' rights" instead of slavery. Groups such as the United Daughters of the Confederacy (founded in 1894) built public monuments that served as tangible reminders of White dominance and chivalry. Most of the monuments built to enshrine Confederate leaders were erected decades after the end of the war, peaking in the years before World War I. Movies, novels, and history books portrayed the War Between the States through this rose-colored glass. Though it has lost much of its potency, the Lost Cause persists today.

> Six million Southern Blacks voted with their feet in the Great Migration (1916-1970) to the Northeast, Midwest, and West. But race prejudice had preceded them. In the 1920s, many cities and towns created restrictive housing covenants that precluded non-White residents or renters in certain neighborhoods. Baltimore's 1911 residential segregation ordinance was the first law to mandate segregation, and although the Supreme Court struck this down a few years later, it set a precedent that continued for decades.

Chapter 15

Repairing What is Broken

A Tale of Two Lawn Mowers

After we launched the BALM ministry in 2018, we struggled to fundraise. Craig Pastor Stan Long had spent almost forty years saying, "I have no needs; how may I serve you?" Now, leading a nonprofit, the message needed to be, "God is doing a great thing in this ministry. Come partner with us!" Voices in Craig's head whispered, "Nobody wants what you're offering. You have nothing to contribute. You're a presumptuous dreamer. BALM is not God's plan. Quit."

After a particularly stressful spring day, Craig stopped by our favorite discount grocery store and saw—to his surprise—lawn mowers for sale. To the amusement of the cashier, he bought two: one for us and one for the BALM office and leadership residence in our old neighborhood. He dropped off one at home and headed to the office to cut the lawn.

When he arrived, he saw our neighbor Mr. Carter across the street, looking troubled. We'd known Mr. Carter since moving to Pen Lucy over thirty years ago, and his children had attended youth group with ours. Strong and wiry even in his 70s, he'd worked full-time as a janitor but always picked up side work: digging, painting, hauling, shoveling snow, and mowing lawns. He'd occasionally borrowed money from Craig to buy medicine for his ailing wife Alice, or repairs for his old truck. He paid back every penny. He insisted on calling me "Miss Maria" even though I told him he could drop the "Miss".

Craig greeted Mr. Carter, who looked down at two old lawnmowers. The rubber tires had shredded off one mower's back wheels, and neither engine worked. "I've done everything I can to get one of them going," Mr. Carter said. "Nothing worked."

Craig felt the Spirit nudge him with Proverbs 3:27: "Do not withhold good from those who deserve it, when it is in your power to act."

Craig nodded sympathetically, and said, "Mr. Carter, can you help me get a box out of my car?"

Mr. Carter followed Craig across the street to his car. When Craig opened the rear door, Mr. Carter's eyes widened. They lifted the box and lumbered into the neighbor's yard. In five minutes, they'd assembled the gleaming new machine. They filled its gas tank, pulled the cord, and the mower purred to life.

"Mr. Carter, could you use this?" Craig asked. "Do you have some jobs lined up?

"Yes, Pastor Craig. I have more jobs than I can get to."

"Well, this lawn mower is for you."

When he realized Craig was giving it to him, not just lending it, he thanked Craig profusely. "I have never had a new lawnmower."

Mr. Carter was stunned by grace. Craig was stunned by the uncanny providence of God. If God could provide a lawnmower for Mr. Carter at the precise moment he needed it, he could surely lead us and provide for BALM.

God invites weak, faltering image-bearers to participate in his divine plan. Paul writes, "We are his workmanship, created in Christ Jesus for good works, which God prepared beforehand, that we should walk in them" (Eph. 2:10). As hard as he'd worked, Mr. Carter had never had the money to buy a decent tool vital to his job. Giving him a lawn mower felt like Christmas to us. But I couldn't stop thinking about all that Mr. Carter could have done if he'd had the resources.

Repentance and Restitution

Nehemiah and other prophets repented for the sins of their ancestors. But is repentance more than a transaction between humans and God? Is there a horizontal element as well? Do we have any responsibility to repair what we or our ancestors have broken?

In the Mosaic law, God called for an outward manifestation of repentance. Because all sin demonstrates our rebellion against our Creator, the offender presented an offering to God. But he also offered restitution to the offended party. Restitution is restoring what has been taken or compensating someone for loss or damage.

A thief acknowledged his guilt and brought an atonement offering to the Lord. He also restored what was stolen and added a fifth (20%) to its value (Lev. 5- 7). Zacchaeus demonstrates this repentance when he vowed to pay back what he'd stolen. Because his heart overflowed with gratitude, he promised not the mandated 20%, but 400%.

Have America's historic racial sins damaged our brothers and sisters of color?

Christianity Today editor Timothy Dalrymple writes:
> Two original sins have plagued this nation from its inception: the destruction of its native inhabitants and the institution of slavery. ... The virus of racism infected our church, our Constitution, and laws, our attitudes, and ideologies. We have never fully defeated it. Slavery was a symptom of the virus, not the virus itself. Even after the abolition of slavery, the ideology that had supported and formed around slavery endured. The symptom passed. The virus persisted by mutating.[1]

Yet Americans remain divided on whether the virus of racism persists. In 2019, only 38% of practicing White Christians said they believed the U.S. has a race problem, compared to 78% of practicing Black Christians.[2] Sixty-one percent of White Christians say that people's own beliefs and prejudices cause them to treat people of other races poorly, while 66% of Black Christians believe racial discrimination is built into our society and institutions.[3]

What do the statistics say? By many measurements—unemployment, academic achievement, health, wealth, and access to home ownership—Black and Brown Americans are not on equal footing with Whites.

- Black unemployment is double that of Whites.
- Black, Latino, and Native American high school students have significantly less access to the full range of math and science courses and attend schools with three times more first-year teachers than White students.[4]
- High-cost loans are offered five times more often in Black neighborhoods than in White ones.[5]
- Mexican Americans experience persistent educational disadvantages, overt discrimination, and income inequality. Darker-skinned Mexican Americans experience more discrimination and stereotyping than those who are lighter-skinned.[6]
- Black and Native American women are three times as likely to die in childbirth as White women.[7]

How should Christians respond to this reality? We balance a seeming paradox: Only Jesus can atone for our sins (good deeds don't save us), yet as his children, our repentance and gratitude to God will show in our good works. These are complementary principles, operating in tandem like the wheels of a bicycle. We are not individually culpable for

> **We can't reduce repentance to merely words; repentance and faith will be seen in changed lives and actions.**

the sins of others, but are responsible if we don't speak out against it. We can't reduce repentance to merely words; repentance and faith will be seen in changed lives and actions. As James writes, "Thus also faith by itself, if it does not have works, is dead." (James 2:17) Our calendars, checkbooks, and choices reflect either our idolatry (anything we value above God) or our obedience.

HISTORY WINDOW 15

World Wars, the Depression, and a New Deal

When 360,000 Black soldiers in World War I returned home, they faced Jim Crow racism anew. Violent racial riots broke out in dozens of cities during the "Red Summer" of 1919. In many cities, White police refused to intervene—or even participated—in the riots. One of these riots, the Tulsa Race Massacre (1921), destroyed the "Black Wall Street" and killed hundreds of Black residents.

While the "social gospel" movement of the 1900s challenged Christians to reform political structures that impoverished many, most conservative Christians were leery of the theological liberalism and rejection of biblical authority that many of its proponents embraced. Other Christians believed the church should steer clear of "worldly" concerns.

During the Great Depression, Southern lawmakers tailored Roosevelt's New Deal of the 1930s and Fair Deal of the 1940s to exclude Black Americans. One historian writes, "At the very moment when a wide array of public policies was providing most White Americans with valuable tools to advance their social welfare—ensure their old age, get good jobs, acquire economic security, build assets, and gain middle-class status—most Black Americans were left behind or left out."[35]

For example, the Federal Housing Administration denied

loans to certain neighborhoods and color-coded lending maps. Neighborhoods with Black residents were coded red, and lenders were unlikely to issue loans in such "risky" neighborhoods. Redlining shaped urban areas across the nation and continued through the 1960s. Restrictive covenants in White neighborhoods excluded selling or renting homes to non-Whites.

The White church largely cooperated with segregation, sometimes turning away non-White worshippers. When a massive shift to the suburbs known as White flight occurred, many churches relocated as well.

Chapter 16

Hospitality

"I've Come From the Pit of Hell": Radical Hospitality

> When you give a dinner or a banquet, do not invite your friends or your brothers or your relatives or rich neighbors, lest they also invite you in return and you be repaid. But when you give a feast, invite the poor, the crippled, the lame, the blind, and you will be blessed, because they cannot repay you. For you will be repaid at the resurrection of the just. Luke 14:12-14

Jesus sets a high bar for hospitality. Don't just invite your friends; host challenging guests who can't pay you back. Invite those who society overlooks or shuns. He promises a blessing. But is that blessing in this life or the next?

After forty years of opening my home, I'd rather invite uncomplicated people who arrive on time, eat what's offered, and express appreciation. I'd rather not host those who arrive two hours late, spend the evening listing my—or my husband's—faults, or wander through the house to pilfer money. Such guests overtax my already-messy life.

If inviting a neighbor for coffee is a stroll in the park and hosting poor or handicapped people is a brisk walk, then sheltering a recovering addict is the Boston Marathon. Addicts will break your heart. And break it again. I've had tenants lie or plead their way into an apartment we owned, only to see their rent money go into their veins. I've seen talented neighbors and church members consumed by addictions. My family tree is shot through with addiction: my grandfather, mother, brother, and nephew.

A few years ago, I offered temporary hospitality to my nephew, Evan. After ten years of opioid addiction, my bright, high-achieving nephew had lost his job, his wife, and his house. He'd stolen my brother's tools and my sister-in-law's jewelry. He'd lived on the street. He'd been kicked out of his parents' home and brought back in for another chance multiple times. He'd exhausted the treatment options in his state.

I knew my hospitality wouldn't fix Evan. But we could give him another chance in a new city and get him into the year-long recovery program at Baltimore's Helping Up Mission. I purged our medicine cabinet of any leftover pills from Craig's back surgery. I hid my wallet. I inspected his suitcase when he arrived. The next day, assisted by our church deacon Carneal, who'd overcome a decades-long crack and alcohol addiction, we drove him to a hospital for detox. After he completed that brief program, we got him into the Helping Up Mission.

Within a week, Evan walked out. He didn't call me; he called my brother, crying and begging, and got a ticket home. A year later, he died in his bed of an overdose.

Would I have taken in Evan after he'd completed the year-long program? Yes. He was family. But two women from our church, Joan and Patty, invited a recovering addict who was not kin, Gloria, to live with them.

Gloria spent twenty-five years bouncing between her mother's house, shelters, treatment centers, and the homes of abusive men. She said she funded her crack habit by "jumpin' into men's cars." Our church's efforts to help Gloria and her son James lasted a decade. At least ten church members—Carneal, elders, deacons, the Women's Committee, a social worker, and a counselor—formed an ad hoc Gloria Care Team. Over and over, we wrestled with how to help rather than enable someone with mental health struggles and long-term addiction. And the boy tumbling in her wake.

We first met Gloria when her five-year-old son James attended our church's after-school recreation league. A volunteer saw that James needed stability and started taking him home after school, helping with homework, and feeding him. At 8:00 or 9:00 p.m., she would take him to where Gloria lived with her boyfriend, who drove James to his grandmother's on the other side of town. The next day it all started up again.

Gloria detoxed at 28-day programs several times but kept relapsing. With no income, her options for long-term treatment were limited. After much thought, prayer, and input, the deacons funded her stay at a twelve-month recovery center. She left after the first day. A year later, we got her into another program. She left that one too.

She bounced in and out of our lives, her contact fueled by need. Gloria knew how to work the system. She would rifle through the church directory and call anyone she knew for money. Carneal confronted her. "I asked her to please stop calling everyone in the directory. She said she only called one other person. Sunday I heard from four other people she had called."

She asked to live in a small apartment the church owned. After deliberation, Carneal emailed the care team. "We've given her plenty of opportunities. Part of recovery is learning to take and follow directions. She has shown none of this. ... I don't think she will heal as long as we keep propping her up." The care team said no.

Finally, Gloria agreed to a year-long rehab. This time, she completed the program. Afterward, she needed stable, drug-free housing. She needed community and growth in faith and life skills. The church leaders approached two single women, Joan Nelson and Patty Prasada-Rao, who shared a three-bedroom apartment nearby. Patty had worked in campus ministry for over a decade and was in her mid-30s; Joan, who worked at Faith, had logged more than twenty years in urban ministry. Could Gloria stay with them for a few months?

They prayed about it and felt God was leading them to say yes. They knew this would be complicated. Patty told me later, "She needed more accountability because of her mental health and addiction, but we didn't want to patronize her. She had to pull her own weight as a roommate, be treated as an equal." This meant doing chores and letting your roommates know if you wouldn't be home that night. Going to work or day programs. Being drug-free.

They emptied out Joan's home office, and Gloria moved in. At some point, Gloria relapsed. Patty recalled, "I remember praying with her, and she would cry when she would fall." Patty said she saw parallels to her own struggles to follow God in hard areas.

Having a challenging roommate forced Patty to deeper self-evaluation and compassion. "We can get good at stuffing away our own vulnerabilities; I had to face mine. I didn't like that I got so frustrated. I wanted to be nicer, kinder. I didn't want to face that I wasn't as patient as I thought I was." She also realized that a challenging roommate was a 24/7 responsibility. "It forced me to not have that safe place to retreat to."

In retrospect, Joan doesn't think the hospitality she and Patty offered was worth noting or unique. "There was a lot of this kind of thing going on at Faith. It seems a shame that it is considered radical hospitality. We just did what we thought we should."

Gloria is 58 now, with her own apartment, a job, and a grandson. She's been clean for a dozen years and effuses gratitude for God, the church, Joan, and Patty. "I've come from the pit of hell. For Patty and Joan not to even know me, and y'all found me a place.... I thank God for all of you. Y'all prayed for me and didn't give up on me. Most of all, God didn't give up on me. I wasn't a [good] mother, but now I'm a good daughter, aunt, and grandmother. God has brought me through some things. God has been good to me."

The radical hospitality Joan and Patty offered is best executed as part of an extended community, like the Gloria Care Team, or a church. It's the SEAL team of hospitality, requiring counsel, support, and stamina.

As they offered Gloria the grace they had received from Christ, Joan and Patty had to keep coming back to Jesus for strength. Their sacrificial love helped Gloria felt seen, heard, and valued. She solidified her recovery. She learned that she, too, had something to offer: her life, her story, her friendship.

Hospitality–Regular and Radical

We sometimes overlook the extraordinary hospitality of the early church: Jews and Gentiles eating together, notorious sinners included among Jesus's key leaders, former political enemies united in faith, enslaved people welcomed in the homes of wealthy fellow believers. This radical hospitality was as cross-cultural then as it is today.

Hospitality is both a command and a gift. Even though he didn't own a home, Jesus practiced hospitality, inviting the outcasts and rejects into his community. Jesus says that when we welcome the poor, the hungry, the stranger, and the prisoner, we are serving him. In ways we may not fully see, we will be blessed.

> **Jesus says that when we welcome the poor, the hungry, the stranger, or the prisoner, we are serving him.**

Setting another place at the table is inconvenient in our task-oriented culture that values productivity and privacy. It's easy to choose achievement over relationships, schedules over interruptions. We fear being overwhelmed, inconvenienced, exhausted.

One of the Greek words used in the New Testament for hospitality is "philoxenia," which means love of strangers. Inviting friends is challenging enough; inviting strangers—an acquaintance from the gym, a friend-of-a-friend who just moved to town, a neighbor you met last week—may feel awkward. We recoil at the security ramifications of such hospitality. We are tempted to make hospitality tame.

Yet I've found people are surprised and pleased, whether it's an invitation to a taco dinner or just dropping off a welcome gift. Once, after I brought homemade muffins to a new neighbor's house, he seemed stunned. "My mother told me that people used to do this. But in all the times we've moved, no one has ever welcomed us to a neighborhood."

Each year, a million international students arrive to study in the U.S., but 75% will never be invited into an American home. Similarly, immigrant families face a dizzying array of new customs, expectations, and bureaucracy, often without someone to help them. How would their lives change if Christians welcomed them?

Rosaria Butterfield, author of *The Gospel Comes with a House Key*, contrasts biblical hospitality with its more secular counterpart. "Entertainment is about impressing people and keeping them at arm's length. Hospitality is about opening up your heart and your home, just as you are, and being willing to invite

Jesus into the conversation, not to stop the conversation but to deepen it."[1]

In welcoming the stranger or the outsider, our worlds expand. We can form friendships that bless both host and guest.

Hospitality and Cultural Disequilibrium

The unity and hospitality called for in the Scripture includes welcoming those who are different from us. "Claims of loving all humankind, of 'welcoming the other' have to be accompanied by the hard work of actually welcoming a human being into a real place."[2]

Crossing these boundaries brings both benefits and challenges. As we explore others' cultural beliefs and values, we are better able to see and critique our own. We can evaluate them through a gospel lens, instead of blindly assuming our own culture is normal. Lesslie Newbigin, British theologian and missiologist, says, "We need help in seeing our own culture through Christian minds shaped by other cultures.... We need the witness of the whole ecumenical family if we are to be authentic witnesses for Christ to our own culture."[3]

Yet crossing cultures can create disequilibrium—a sense of losing one's footing. We can feel out of place, ignorant, or insecure. Disequilibrium can happen within one's own race, or when crossing race/class boundaries. How do we respond to this? The following graph illustrates two possibilities. We may react by feeling self-righteous, defensive, or disrespectful. Or we can respond in a gospel-centered way.

Openness Humility Acceptance Trust Adaptability	→	Understanding, empathy, deepening relationships "I had no idea. Thanks for explaining that." "Tell me more. What do you mean?" "I noticed you did x... can you explain that to me?" "How interesting! That [tradition] shows how you value family. I appreciate that." "Now that you've explained the history of that tradition, it seems like a beautiful way to dignify the image of God in everyone."
Suspicion Fear Superiority Prejudice Criticism Withdrawing	→	Alienation, broken relationships, stagnation "That's the thanks I get for attempting to reach out. I'm done." "I can't believe he took my comment that way!" "Those people are thieves. Lock your cars in that neighborhood." "That's a weird way to observe a holiday! "I don't get that at all! Makes no sense." "What did she mean by that? I'm done!"

HISTORY WINDOW 16

Post-World War II America

Post-war government programs designed to foster the American Dream—a good education, quality employment, and home ownership—actually widened the gap between White and Black Americans. The G.I. Bill (1944), which propelled many veterans into the middle class with educational and housing supports, "was deliberately designed to accommodate Jim Crow."[36] States administrating these programs often discriminated against African Americans; for example, of the first 67,000 mortgages insured, fewer than 100 were taken out by non-Whites. Many banks refused loans to Blacks or issued only higher-interest mortgages with excessively punitive provisions. The Veteran's Administration denied mortgages to Black soldiers and often steered them into lower-level training and education rather than four-year colleges. Many colleges still refused to admit Black applicants, and HBCUs (Historically Black Colleges and Universities) couldn't absorb all the applicants.

In the 1970s, well-paying manufacturing and industry jobs began to disappear as jobs moved overseas. U.S. manufacturing employment has declined significantly, replaced by lower-paying service-sector jobs.[37, 38] Deindustrialization cut off the path to the middle class for Americans of all races, but especially for minorities who are often the "last hired, first fired."

Finally, the dramatic rise in mass incarceration since the 1980s has had catastrophic consequences for minorities and cities. The war on drugs, a series of federal directives to fight the drug epidemic, disproportionally punished Black and Brown people. The U.S. now has one of the highest rates of incarceration in the world and holds more than 2 million people in prisons and jails—a 500% increase over the last forty years. This increase is due to changes in policy and sentencing law, not changes in crime rates.[39]

Was the church a prophetic voice calling attention to these injustices? Some individuals and churches responded by creating nonprofits to minister to prisoners, the poor, or those struggling with addiction. But the need outstripped demand, and few churches or denominations addressed systemic roots of these problems.

Chapter 17

A Harder Bridge to Cross

Straddling the Socioeconomic Divide

As a child, I once asked my father, "Are we rich or poor?" I'd encountered both in my storybooks: impoverished street urchins and pampered princesses; poor orphans and wealthy little lords. But because of zoning laws, my neighbors were, like us, middle class. I attended an excellent public school with children whose parents worked upper-level government or business jobs.

Poverty—or even financial hardship—existed elsewhere, out of sight. Only in high school did we move to another state, where my circle include less privileged friends: one lived in a trailer park, another in a rented, run-down house with junk in the yard.

Though I often had no cash in college, I wasn't poor. My parents paid my tuition and would have bailed me out of any significant money woes. My immediate needs were met, so I had the luxury of continuing my middle-class mindset: plan for the future, make short-term sacrifices to yield long-term gains.

I was not prepared for the culture shock of moving to a lower-income area at age 22. Poverty pressed down, stifling and omnipresent like Baltimore's August heat. I couldn't unsee the bitter fruit of decades of segregation, redlining, discrimination, and economic disparity.

Growing up, our children navigated being both poor and rich. They watched, embarrassed, as their parents salvaged furniture that others put out for bulk trash. They scoured thrift stores for clothes. They babysat and mowed lawns to buy beat-up cars to get to after-school jobs. One daughter, who attended an expensive high school on scholarship, drove an old Camry that stopped going in reverse. For a few weeks, she had to push it out of its parking space next to her classmates' new Hondas and Volvos.

But in the neighborhood, we appeared rich: we owned our house. We had cars, electricity, and heat. We ate dinner together. The kids attended private or Christian schools. We had a week at the beach every summer, funded by grandparents. Our shelves were crammed with books. Our good teeth telegraphed privilege.

As they straddled the socioeconomic divide, our children learned to work hard, practice frugality, and be comfortable with different types of people. We knew that unlike many neighbors mired in generational poverty, we had options. Craig could quit the pastorate and restart his prior career. I could stop volunteering, pay for day care, and get a "real" job (which I eventually did to pay school tuitions). We could—and did—start a side job (what Christians call "tentmaking," after the Apostle Paul's profession), to supplement our income.

Learning from those who are poor in their pocketbooks but rich in faith challenged me. Would I, like one church family, adopt three preteen nephews in crisis when their own family was barely getting by? Would I give quietly and generously despite my need, not from my surplus? Would I, like my immigrant friends, subsist on one minimum-wage paycheck and do without a car or smartphone to send money to my church back home? People who pray "give us this day our daily bread," and mean it inspire awe.

The socioeconomic gap is a harder bridge to cross than race. When I bridge that divide, I face uncomfortable questions. Do I feel guilty about my wealth when my on-the-cusp-of-homelessness immigrant friend visits for tea? Do I tell you how God miraculously provided my renovated kitchen to give him praise, or to assuage my guilt? I'm challenged to reflect on God's values, not the world's. I'm forced to admit I'd rather trust my bank balance than God's provision.

The socioeconomic gap I saw in my urban neighborhood is part of the profound wealth gap that exists between White, Black, and Latinx families. Wealth— defined as assets minus liabilities— predicts whether families can respond to financial challenges like layoffs, health crises, or family emergencies. According to a Yale University study, "People estimated that for every $100 in wealth held by a White family, a Black family has $90, when in reality, that Black family has $10. For Latinx American families the estimate was $75, while in reality it is around $9.50. And for Asian American families the estimate was $95, and the reality is around $85."[1] When Craig and I were low on funds, we could turn to our relatives or get a home equity line of credit. But in many low-income families, the extended family is short on cash, and "payday loans" charge exorbitant interest.

This vast misperception of the wealth gap lulls people into inaction. "As long as most Americans believe society is pretty much equal and things are fair, any effort at change will be met with resistance." The researchers conclude that "There are no true explanations of the wealth gap that don't rest in racism."[2]

Truth be told, I have more in common with my professional, African American or Korean friends than I do with White high school dropouts who work at McDonalds. Yet if we unite around Jesus, we share a powerful, transcending bond.

Wealth, Poverty, and the Kingdom of God

In the Bible study for this chapter, we will examine Old and New Testament teachings about wealth, poverty, and preferential treatment on the basis of wealth.

In the Old Testament, God revealed through Moses the righteousness he wanted. Every festival or celebration of his goodness included a reminder to remember the poor, such as the immigrant and the fatherless. He set up the Year of Jubilee every fifty years to free the enslaved. Israel's obedience would demonstrate to other nations that they were a people set apart, the people of God.

This same concern for justice and the poor is woven throughout the New Testament. Jesus equates caring for the poor with caring for him (Matt. 25). James tells us not to give preferential treatment to the wealthy (James 2). When Paul and

Barnabas are commissioned to bring the gospel to the Gentiles, the other apostles urged them "to remember the poor, the very thing I was eager to do" (Gal. 2).

Jesus spoke a great deal about money. He told his followers to give to the needy without looking for human acclaim. He urged them to lay up treasures in heaven, "for where your treasure is, there your heart will be also" (Matt. 6:19-21). Contrary to the common misquote that "money is the root of all evil," the Bible teaches that overvaluing money can lead to evil behavior. "The love of money is a root of all kinds of evils." Paul tells his younger disciple Timothy, "Godliness with contentment is great gain, for we brought nothing into the world, and we cannot take anything out of the world. But if we have food and clothing, with these we will be content" (1 Tim. 6:6-7,8).

Paul tells the saints at Philippi that he has learned to be content whatever the circumstances, whether hard-pressed or well-provisioned, because Jesus strengthens him (Phil. 4:12-13). He urges the Corinthians to give generously (1 Cor. 8:1-15). He repeats this instruction in the next chapter, reminding the saints that "God loves a cheerful giver" (2 Cor. 9:6-7).

> Following Jesus isn't about my material comfort. It's about loving Jesus, glorifying God and enjoying Him forever.

When oil magnate John D. Rockefeller was once asked, "How much money is enough?" he answered, "Just a little bit more." As imperfect Christians in a fallen world, we can fall prey to the lure of "just a little bit more" or be trapped by "the snare of compare."

Some best-selling spirituality books focus on what God can do for me: apparently, he's eager to make me healthy and wealthy now. But following Jesus isn't about my material comfort. It's not about piling up material wealth. It's about loving Jesus and following him. It's about glorifying God and enjoying him forever.[3]

HISTORY WINDOW 17

The Church and the Civil Rights Era

We'd like to believe that the American church was an unflagging advocate of equal rights during the Civil Rights Era. Yet this perspective "may be somewhat skewed. Precious few Christians publicly aligned themselves with the struggle for black freedom. ...Those who did faced backlash."[40] In his 2004 memoir of the Civil Rights Movement in his small Southern town, historian Timothy Tyson states that it was not White civil rights advocates who spearheaded change. "Black Southerners ... toppled the American racial caste system."[41]

Unbiblical theologies of sin and segregation played a role in thwarting racial justice. Religious conservatives tended to view sin as solely individual choice. Yet a more robust, biblical understanding recognizes that sin also infects the systems we create. Some Christians, especially in the South, saw segregation as God's design and feared that integration would lead to intermarriage. (Of course, fear of miscegenation, or race mixing, had not deterred numerous White slaveholders from sexually exploiting enslaved Black women).

Evangelical response to the Civil Rights Movement was mixed. In 1952, Billy Graham refused to preach to segregated meetings in the South and removed ropes that separated White and Black seating areas. A few years later, he invited Martin

Luther King Jr. to pray at one of his rallies. Yet many White Christians failed to support the Civil Rights Movement, and King wrote his famous "Letter from a Birmingham Jail" (1963) to address them. When the Civil Rights Act of 1964 was passed, and many conservative Christians protested, Graham didn't denounce or commend the law—a decision he later regretted.

While some mainstream or liberal religious organizations publicly spoke in favor of it, the National Association of Evangelicals (NAE) refused to take a stand, concluding that civil rights was not the business of the church. Integration led to a widespread exit from public schools and spawned many segregated White Christian academies. One very conservative school, Bob Jones University in Greenville, South Carolina, refused to admit Black students until 1971 and prohibited interracial dating until 2000. Finally, in 2008, the university admitted that its policies were wrong.

Chapter 18

Partnering with God in Restoration
Worthy

Will we ever see the unity Jesus prayed for in John 17? Will we experience united worship from "every tribe and language and people and nation" that the Apostle John describes in Revelation 7?

We will.

We do.

When Craig stepped down as pastor of Faith Christian Fellowship after 38 years, we promised to stay away as the new pastor settled in. We have seen former pastors remain and inadvertently make life harder for the new leader. But after six months, we returned to Faith's annual Advent Concert as guests.

For decades, the Advent Concert has been a jaw-dropping blend of genres, readings, and original compositions. The church's musical talent is out of proportion to congregational size, inflated by students and graduates of Peabody Conservatory and other Baltimore universities: cellists, pianists, flutists, composers.

Classical duos and gospel-music trios. An ethnic-rainbow children's choir, with its inevitable stage-fright-frozen tot or wildly enthusiastic heart-stealer. A bluegrass quartet updating an old hymn. African and hip-hop Christmas carols. An original narrative by a novelist. A poetry recitation from a polymath special-education teacher. Yet this is not just a showcase of rarefied talent: thinner voices shine when surrounded with harmonies, and choppy guitarists when supported by expert violinists. All are welcome.

"How does this happen?" visitors ask. The concert hasn't been the handiwork of one music minister, choir director, or committee, but a shifting cast of men and women. It's both spectacular and ordinary: God's diverse people, bringing their best.

As I watched a combined choir sing "Is He Worthy?" by composer Andrew Peterson, the wounds and weariness of decades of ministry shifted toward healing. The song, based on Revelation 5-7, looks to when God will make all things new, when people from every tribe, nation, and tongue will worship together. I wept openly as men, women, and children I've known and loved for years—people from hardscrabble 'hoods and affluent enclaves, Chad and Nigeria and Kenya and Cuba—sang Peterson's call-and-response hymn about the brokenness of the world, the persistence of the Light breaking in, and the beauty of Jesus. (If you don't know this song, watch it on YouTube.)

Jesus is worthy—of the years when we wondered if this church would take root, because experts told us multiethnic congregations don't work. When it did grow, we wondered if the next crisis would blow the whole thing up. We felt our inadequacy constantly, never being able to do enough. We listened to women shattered by abuse, and stood by the caskets of gunshot victims. We mourned at the bedside of a mother whose newborn would soon gasp her last breath. I worried about my preoccupied, exhausted husband, and about how living in our neighborhood, or being "the pastor's kids," would affect our children.

Yet I got to see the church demonstrate the firstfruits of this All-Things-Made- New vision: every tribe and nation worshipping in community. Imperfect, but together. Damaged souls, all of us, but being made new every day. I saw it more clearly than I had as the pastor's wife, when I skimmed over moments like this to address the next crisis.

Maybe it wasn't our job to fix all the broken people, to comfort every mourner, to figure out how to help yet one more person pay the electric bill. To make sure every church program functioned, every sermon spoke to PhDs and high school dropouts and teenagers. That music and worship and sermon illustrations spoke to Blacks and Whites and Hispanics and residents from all of Baltimore.

Maybe I should have lingered in the mystery. Accepted the fact that we see glimpses, never the full restoration. Like the Apostle Paul, who later in life wrote of himself as the "chief of sinners," I am fractured and sin-steeped in ways both visible and invisible. But God delights in redeeming what is broken. Jesus is not only worthy of our devotion and unity, but he also makes it possible. Jesus is worthy of all this.

The Restoration of God

As we have seen, the gospel has both lateral and vertical dimensions: it reconciles us to God, but also to each other. The more I dwell in God's love, and in my identity as his beloved child, the more I can embrace God's gospel imperative to live as a united, diverse community.

Living in community impacts how we see God's heart for justice. Dr. Irwyn Ince writes, "Devoting ourselves to the doctrine of unity in diversity as a gospel imperative will compel us to press into issues of justice, racism, and oppression.... We will also embrace the gospel call to repair and restore as fruit of our repentance."[1]

> The more I dwell in God's love, the more I can embrace God's gospel imperative to live as a united, diverse community.

God is reweaving the torn fabric of society through his people, the church.

This is our job description. We are his "workmanship" (masterpiece, Greek poiema), "created in Christ Jesus for good works, which God prepared beforehand, that we should walk in them" (Eph. 2:10). These good works don't earn our salvation, but rather demonstrate it. God is using us in his restoration project.

We live in "the now and not yet"—the time between the first and second coming of Christ. He commissions us to make disciples of all nations, be his hands and feet, and partner with him. He will ultimately return to usher in a new heaven and new earth. Until then, we are called to do justly, love kindness, and walk humbly with our God (Mic. 6:8).

Is Critical Race Theory the Answer to Brokenness?

Is Critical Race Theory (CRT) a step forward in bringing God's shalom to a sin-damaged society? It is a tool for analysis, but it is not the remedy.

Definitions of CRT are ever-evolving, and adherents of this theory embrace different tenets and applications. One Christian scholar points out that CRT "is not a single theory, method, or analytic tool. It's a diverse, contested, multi-layered movement."[2] As believers in Jesus, we evaluate each aspect through the lens of Scripture.

CRT grew out of academic Critical Theory studies in law in the 1970s, but has now flowed into education, theology, government, and popular discussion.

Based on a humanistic, Marxist framework, CRT believes that racism is a pervasive problem requiring significant structural reform. Our gender, race, and sexual orientation are our primary, defining characteristics. CRT views people through the lens of intersectionality, or the intersections of race, gender, sexual orientation, and gender identity. People are either oppressed or oppressors, depending on these characteristics. Those with the most power—which historically in the U.S. is White, straight males—are unable to adequately see reality because of their privileged state. The solution is for them to give up power and listen to previously marginalized voices.

How do these theories align with a biblical worldview? In general, CRT oversimplifies issues, denies human sinfulness, and provides inadequate solutions. Theologian and professor Dr. Anthony Bradley says CRT is ultimately "a reductionistic theory of human evil and suffering. ... It is woefully inadequate to explain the nature of reality."[3]

Christians agree that racism, like all sin, is a result of the Fall. We see wreckage of racism globally, and in America. Our history is filled with both blatant and subtle policies and events that have ensured the social and economic dominance of White Americans. But often, these events have been downplayed or ignored in the way history is taught, so that many Americans remain unaware of them.

Western Christians tend to view sin through an individualistic lens, but the Bible calls us to consider corporate and generational sin as well. Christians are to recognize, repent, and (to the extent possible) make amends. The gospel offers grace and renewal to us as we turn from sin in repentance. By applying the gospel to the historic sins of racism and oppression, we participate in God's plan of restoration that will ultimately be fulfilled in Christ's return.

In considering the idea of intersectionality, we recognize that "various types of structural sin can intersect in ways that cause a 'multiplier effect.'"[4] Yet CRT falls short in its solutions, and can create hierarchies of victimization. It "can be used to promote the flourishing of the human community or ...to create new forms of systematic sin... the concept has frequently... been used as a tool for building division ...between the "oppressors" (i.e., White males) and the oppressed (i.e., almost everyone else)".[5]

Ultimately, the solutions offered by CRT are inadequate. "CRT is attempting to give an account of evil and salvation. ... Instead of the resurrection of Jesus Christ, CRT simply wants to dismantle racism in an attempt to achieve cosmic salvation. ... Anti-racism will set us free."[6]

In summary, Dr. Bradley offers a nuanced perspective on evaluating CRT. "As a covenant theologian, I need not wholly accept or reject secular frameworks for understanding reality. I can eat the meat and spit out the bones."[7]

Tenets of CRT	Biblical Worldview
Draws on tenets of Karl Marx to explain the world.	Based on God's revelation in Scripture and Jesus Christ.
Systemic racism exists and is created by socioeconomic forces.	Like all sin, racism begins in the heart. (Gen. 3; Rom. 5). Because of the Fall, we will build unjust systems. "If sinners build a society, that society will be structured in ways that reinforce whatever sins dominate the hearts of those who build it.... Generations later, those structures might still perpetuate the problems."[8]
Injustice is due to unjust social structures and systems.	Attributes injustice to multiple factors, including social, environmental, spiritual, and individual causes. It doesn't dismiss individual responsibility.

Tenets of CRT	Biblical Worldview
Marx believed that power exists, and people use it to oppress others.	Often true; see Pharaoh, Nebuchadnezzar, etc. God established laws to restrict the depravity of man and his use of power; six of God's Ten Commandments deal with how we treat others. In the "Greatest Commandment," Jesus paired loving God and loving others. Jesus gave up his power to serve, and he is our model (Phil. 2:6).
We are either oppressed or oppressors.	Oppression exists (Rom. 3:23), but this binary structure of CRT is reductionistic. It overlooks individual choices, life situations, and the role of evil.
Our gender, race, and sexual orientation are our primary, defining characteristics.	Our defining characteristic is that we're made in the image of God. Our primary identity is that we are children of God, both fallen and beloved. However, we are deeply shaped by our gender, race, background, etc.
Guilt is not assigned on the basis of individual actions but on the basis of group membership and social/racial status.[9]	"The reasons for evil and for unjust outcomes in life are multiple and complex."[10] We bear some responsibility for corporate sin: I am sometimes responsible for and involved in other people's sins (Dan. 9; 2 Sam. 21; 1 Sam. 15:2; Deut. 23:3-8; Josh. 7). Yet I bear individual responsibility for my sins.
Power must be viewed through the lens of "intersectionality" or the intersections of race, gender, sexual orientation, and gender identity.	We are influenced by our race, ethnicity, gender, and sexual orientation, but why stop there? We're also influenced by our culture, subculture, age, etc. God determined the times and places we would live (Acts 17:26).

Tenets of CRT	Biblical Worldview
CRT can create sub-genres of victimization, which often compete for victimhood.	Our identity comes from our adoption as God's children because of Jesus. Though our lived experiences are vastly different, all humans are equal in dignity and value.
Those who are oppressed (more powerless) have greater moral authority and can see "truth" correctly.	CRT is "deeply incoherent" because you "cannot insist that all morality is culturally constructed and relative and then claim that your moral claims are not".[11] This view doesn't take humanity's sin nature into account.
Those with more power, social standing, wealth, etc., are blinded by their privilege and must give up their power.	"Christianity does not merely fill the top rungs of authority with new parties who will use power in the same oppressive way that is the way of the world."[12] Jesus used his power to serve.
Power is exercised by language or truth claims. "Traditional liberal emphasis on individual human rights is an obstacle to the radical changes society will need to undergo in order to share wealth and power."[13]	"Reasoned debate and 'freedom of speech' therefore is out—it only gives unjust discourses airtime. The only way to reconstruct reality in a just way is to subvert dominant discourses— and this requires control of speech."[14]

Tenets of CRT	Biblical Worldview
Our identity or "wokeness" is based on our performance. Are we sufficiently anti-racist? Tends to self-righteousness.	Our Christian identity is not based on our actions, but on Jesus's righteousness attributed to us. We pursue biblical justice and righteousness, but we are not saved by our works (Eph. 2:8).
Society needs radical restructuring. Some proponents of CRT believe this includes redistribution of wealth.	Our wealth belongs to God, and we are only stewards. We should be radically, voluntarily generous. This is neither a capitalist nor socialist view.

HISTORY WINDOW 18

Where Are We Now?

In retrospect, we lament that most White believers were blind to the consequences of racially unjust systems. Were Christians more shaped by culture than the Scriptures?

Do we have similar blind spots today? Do we have the spiritual fortitude to examine this history and respond with lament, rather than defensiveness?

God repeatedly reminded Israel of its past, both as a remembrance of his grace and a cautionary tale of the wreckage of sin. Similarly, America must confront its past. In *Blood Done Sign My Name*, historian Timothy Tyson writes,

> What the advocates of our dangerous and deepening social amnesia don't understand is how deeply the past holds the future in its grip—even, and perhaps especially, when it remains unacknowledged. We are runaway slaves from our own past, and only by turning to face the hounds can we find our freedom beyond them.[43]

Some denominations, including the Southern Baptists and the Presbyterian Church in America, have issued public apologies for race-based sin and established funds for theological training or internships for people of color. Higher education institutions, such as Princeton and Georgetown University, have unflinchingly faced past involvement in enslavement and segregation and pursued "a path of memorialization and reconciliation."[44] May God's people lead the way in pursuing God's call to justice, mercy, and righteousness.

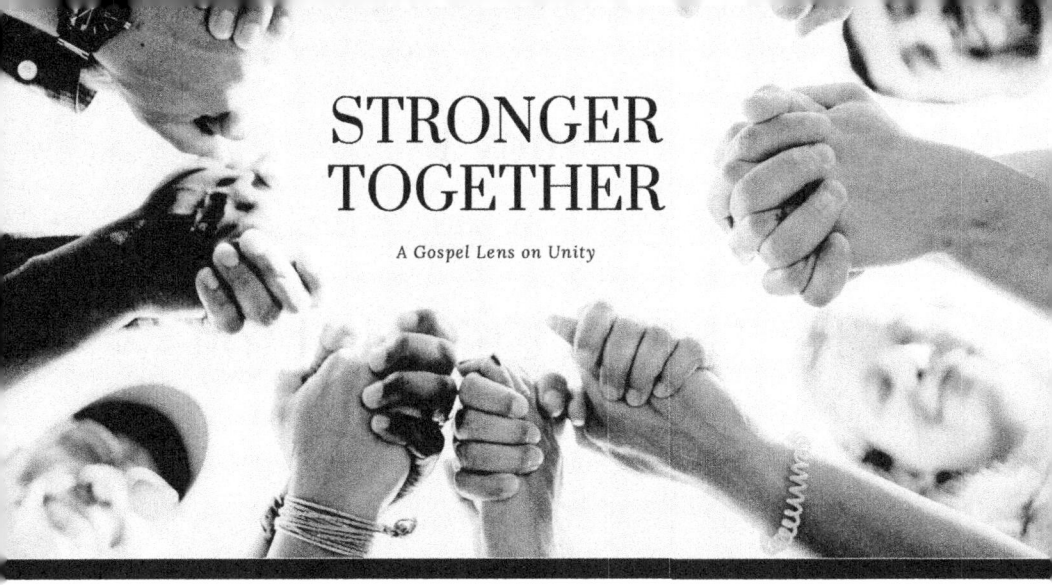

Bible Study & Discussion Guide

Study 1

The Gospel, Unity, and You

Open

1. If you are participating in this study with others, introduce yourself. Share why you are interested in growing in your understanding of Christian unity. What do you hope to gain from this study?

2. Self-reflection is vital in our quest to grow in maturity and unity. How does paying attention to one's own thoughts, behaviors, and emotions help us apply Scripture to life?

Reflect on Scripture

The Great Commission: Matt. 28:18-20
1. Jesus's final command to his disciples is called the Great Commission, not the Great Suggestion. How does the Great Commission relate to the idea of unity?

2. What challenges do you feel as you read this text? What encouragements are embedded in the passage?

Jesus Prays for Unity: John 17:20-23

This passage is pivotal in understanding the importance of unity. On the eve of his crucifixion, like a high priest in the Old Testament, Jesus intercedes with the Father on behalf of the people.

1. Why is it significant that Jesus compares our unity as believers to his unity with his Father and the Spirit?

2. What promises do we find in this passage?

Discuss the quote from this chapter: "The best testimony to the truth of the gospel is the quality of our life together. Jesus risked his reputation and the credibility of his story by tying them to how his followers live and care for one another in community." (Christine Pohl, *Living into Community: Cultivating Practices that Sustain Us*)

Ideas for Follow-Up

1. Keep a journal to record your thoughts about this study. Use your journal to respond to this lesson.

2. When did you first become aware of different cultures in childhood? For our next meeting, share your first interactions with someone of a different culture or background.

Study 2

The Gospel Frees Us

Open

How would you define "the gospel" or good news about Jesus to someone who had never heard of him?

Consider

1. What are some practical applications of Luther's statement that we are simul justus et peccator (simultaneously justified and sinners)? How do we see this in our lives?

2. People are often uncomfortable talking about racial or ethnic bias because the discussion can bring up feelings of guilt, anger, or shame. Do you feel any of these emotions? How does the gospel address our guilt, anger, and shame?

Reflect on Scripture

Read and respond to the following verses, which summarize the gospel.

Rom 8:1 No Condemnation for those in Christ

1. How does this verse apply to my daily life? To my struggle against selfishness and sin?

2. How does it apply to my pursuit of cross-cultural understanding and unity?

God Justifies: Rom. 8:31-34

1. What is the basis for my freedom from sin and condemnation?

2. Why should it encourage me that Jesus is advocating and interceding for me at this moment?

I Don't Care If You Judge Me: 1 Cor. 4:3-4

1. Paul says he doesn't care if people judge him. Do you? Why or why not?

2. What does Paul mean by saying that though his conscience is clear, he might not be innocent?

The Righteousness of God: 2 Cor. 5:21

1. After reading these verses, how would you define the gospel?

2. How would my life be different if I fully believed the gospel right now?

The gospel flies in the face of our desire to "do it my way" or earn our way into God's favor. It is bad news because I must admit that I am so sinful and broken that I can't do enough good works to impress God or deserve to have him love me. But it's supremely good news because it means God sees the depth of my sin yet loves me anyway as I turn to him in faith and repentance!

- We live in daily repentance and faith, returning again and again to the gospel. Gal. 3:3 says, "Are you so foolish? Having begun by the Spirit, are you now being perfected by the flesh?"

- Our sanctification is an ongoing application of the gospel. Sanctification is also by grace, not by works. As we keep in step with the Spirit, we are gradually being transformed and more like what God intended and declares us to be. Colossians 2:6 says, "Therefore, as you received Christ Jesus as Lord, so walk in him."

Activity: Preparing Our Hearts to Engage

These questions were adapted from material from Wellsprings Consulting to encourage deeper self-understanding, Christ-understanding, and care for one another. They are helpful to review before any challenging meeting or interaction. Review the list and discuss why this tool might be especially helpful in intercultural relationships. This is adapted from Shari Thomas and Tami Resch's book *Beyond Duct Tape*.

Preparing Our Hearts

READY TO REPENT • READY TO WAIT • READY TO LISTEN

1. READY TO REPENT

- Am I ready to see and repent as God reveals my prideful heart and judgmental thoughts?

- Am I ready to see and repent of my junk and my idolatrous God substitutes?

- Am I ready to see and repent of wrong motives that drive my interactions?

When my heart refuses to admit and repent of my sin, I will see myself as better than others. My heart will be smug and condescending, which will weaken my effectiveness through unloving, self-righteous words and attitudes.

2. READY TO WAIT

- Is my spirit quiet so I can be a non-anxious, safe presence?
- Do I believe that God (and not me) will rescue the person I'm meeting with?

When I don't assume a posture of waiting on God, I will be impatient to "fix" others.

3. READY TO LISTEN

Listening to God:

- How is God pursuing me? How is God pursuing the person I'm meeting with?
- Am I looking and listening for God to show up?

When my heart refuses to listen to God, I will frantically feel the need to provide an answer. I will feel the weight of responsibility upon my shoulders to be wise.

Listening to Others:

- Am I ready to hear this person's story and ask follow-up questions, rather than talking about myself and my experiences?
- Do I see this person as truly created in the image of God with value and beauty?

> **"Being heard is so close to being loved that for the average person, they are almost indistinguishable."**

Ideas for Follow-Up

1. When (and why) is it hard for you to apply the gospel to your own heart in conversations about race and culture? Write about this in your journal.

2. Make a Top Ten List of what the gospel is and a Top Ten List of what the gospel is not. For example, the gospel is based on grace, not my works. The gospel is not limited to people of a certain ethnic background.

Study 3

The Gospel Unites Us

Open

In this study, we'll discover what the Bible teaches about unity. How did Jesus demonstrate a commitment to unity among diverse people? Even though his ministry took place within Israel, how did he reach out to people of different cultures? What biblical passages do you know that deal with the unity of all believers regardless of race, nationality, ethnicity, and other barriers?

Cleansing the Temple: Mark 11:15-18 and John 2:13-17

1. What do these passages about the cleansing of the temple teach us about God?

2. Do you share Jesus's anger when people are excluded from worshipping God on the basis of race, ethnicity, or social standing? Are there aspects of your worship traditions or practices that might inadvertently contribute to such exclusion?

Jesus's First Sermon: Luke 4:16-27

1. Zarephath was a Phoenician city near Tyre and Sidon. What was Jesus's intention in highlighting the widow in Zarephath? What does this passage reveal about Jesus?

2. How does Jesus's first sermon illustrate his plan to save people from every people group? How did his audience react? Have you considered the multicultural aspect of these verses before?

Activity

Your "lens" influences how you see yourself, others, the church, the world, and the Bible, not by our culture, the media, etc. But we are more complicated than that!

Understanding what has shaped our lens and our cultural beliefs is an important first step in pursuing unity across cultural differences. List some of the factors that influence the way you see the world.

Ideas for Follow-Up

1. Watch one of the "Race and the Church" videos at https://raceandthechurch.com and respond in your journal. Share what you learned with someone.

2. Visit a historical site or museum where you can learn about a different culture or ethnic group.

Study 4

Jesus, the Barrier Breaker

Open

In this study, we focus on how Jesus intentionally ministered to those outside the Jewish mainstream.

Consider

Jesus's disciples were reluctant to go to Samaria and other areas where many non-Jews lived. What places in your community might you be reluctant to visit?

Reflect on Scripture
Read and respond to the following verses.

Jesus and the Samaritan Woman: John 4:1-42

1. Women usually went to the well to draw water early in the morning, not at midday. Why might she have come at this time?

2. What do we learn about Jesus in this passage?

3. How might crossing a cultural barrier bring about transformation in your life?

Jesus and the Syro-Phoenician Woman: Matt. 15:21-28 (parallel passage is Mark 7:24-30)

1. We know that Jesus is not cruel or racist and that God is "no respecter of persons" (Acts 10:34, Rom. 2:11). Why do you think Jesus initially ignores this woman, then draws her out?

2. What do we learn about people in this passage?

3. Read these passages in *The Message,* a Bible paraphrase. How does the author translate Matthew 15:24?

Bible scholar Dr. Jack Beck writes that Jesus came to the region of Tyre and Sidon not only to heal this woman's daughter but also "to show that even in a place that had produced the likes of Jezebel, extraordinary faith could be found."[1] Where (and among what people) do we sometimes not expect to find faith?

Activity

Discuss the differences between race and ethnicity.

Race	Ethnicity
• The idea that humans are divided into groups based on inherited physical differences such as skin color, hair, etc. • Socially imposed, hierarchical	• A group that shares a common, distinctive culture, language, religion, language, or traditions based on historic geographic origins and shared experience • Related to culture; often confused with nationality, but not the same

"Race becomes institutionalized in a way that has profound social consequences on the members of different groups."[2]

Ideas for Follow-Up

1. People from the dominant Anglo culture in the U.S. have been known to say, "We don't have a culture—not like you all do!" What does this statement reveal? How would you respond to it?

2. View and discuss this video clip, "Your English is perfect!" https://www.youtube.com/watch?v=DWynJkN5HbQ

Study 5

Culture and God's Story

Open

How would you define culture?

Activity

Let's consider the concept of culture. Read through each of the following examples and check whether each observance feels "right" or "wrong" in your experience.

Is It Culturally Appropriate in Your Church?	Y	N
1. When we meet for discipleship, my friend is usually 30 minutes late.		
2. The pianist/organist plays music quietly during the pastor's prayer.		
3. People nod their heads but don't speak out loud to affirm the preacher's points during the sermon.		
4. Church services last one hour.		
5. People wear their "Sunday best" to church.		
6. People worship with their bodies—clapping, swaying, or dancing in place.		
7. For a men's activity, the guys went to a shooting range and then had a beer at someone's house.		
8. Real wine is served at communion.		
9. Almost all songs are written by people of White European ethnicity.		
10. The sermon illustrations/quotes frequently cite people of other races.		

1. What questions did this exercise raise for you? What insights?

2. Which questions sparked Scriptural defenses, or objections, in your mind?

Reflect on Scripture

The Creation, Fall, Redemption, and Restoration (CFRR) paradigm answers the questions people across all cultures ask: How did it all start? What went wrong? How will it get fixed? How will it end? These questions form the structure of much storytelling, whether in movies, novels, or folk tales.

Read and respond to the following verses, which correspond to the Creation, Fall, Redemption, and Restoration paradigm.

Creation
God Creates Humankind: Gen. 1:26-31
Chosen in Him: Eph 1:4-5

1. What are the implications of being created in the image of God?

2. What did God provide in creation? Do we still have these needs and longings?

Fall
No One Righteous: Rom. 3:10-12, 23
All Creation Affected: Rom. 8:22-23

For a full account of the Fall, read Genesis 3.

1. How has the Fall affected creation? How has it affected us?

2. List some of the consequences of our sin.

Redemption
Christ Redeemed Us: Gal. 3:13
A Redeemer: Rom. 3:23-25

1. Can you restate this in your own words?

Restoration
A New Heaven and Earth: Rev. 21:1-5
The Heavenly Jerusalem: Rev. 22:1-5

1. The Apostle John describes the vision God shows him of the new heaven and earth. What do you see about creation, about humans, about God, and about our relationships with God and each other?

2. As we look at the four stages of Creation, Fall, Redemption, and Restoration, which stage(s) do we live in? How might this affect our relationships across race, ethnicity, and culture?

Revelation shows the fulfillment of God's plan to gather his people and live with them in the "new heaven and new earth." God restores our relationship with him, with each other, and with creation. Author J.R.R. Tolkien captures this idea in *The Return of the King* with the phrase "everything sad is going to come untrue."

We live in the period between Jesus's first coming and his second coming, when he will make all things new. We are justified sinners who live in a broken world that is being redeemed. Amazingly, God uses his people in this process of re-creation.

The Cultural Iceberg

We often don't realize we have a culture until it's changed or challenged. The first step in growing in cultural intelligence is learning more about one's own culture.

Many of our preferences are shaped by culture and determined by our experiences, backgrounds, ethnic group, geographical region, denomination, etc. Culture is like an iceberg: we generally only see what's above the surface (objective culture). Food, holidays, dress, music, and literature are easily observed and enjoyed by those outside the culture. Subjective culture is less obvious, but just as important. For example, how does this culture view childrearing? What are its ideals of beauty? How are the aged viewed? The less visible, subjective aspects of culture make crossing cultures more challenging. Discuss the Cultural Iceberg image below.

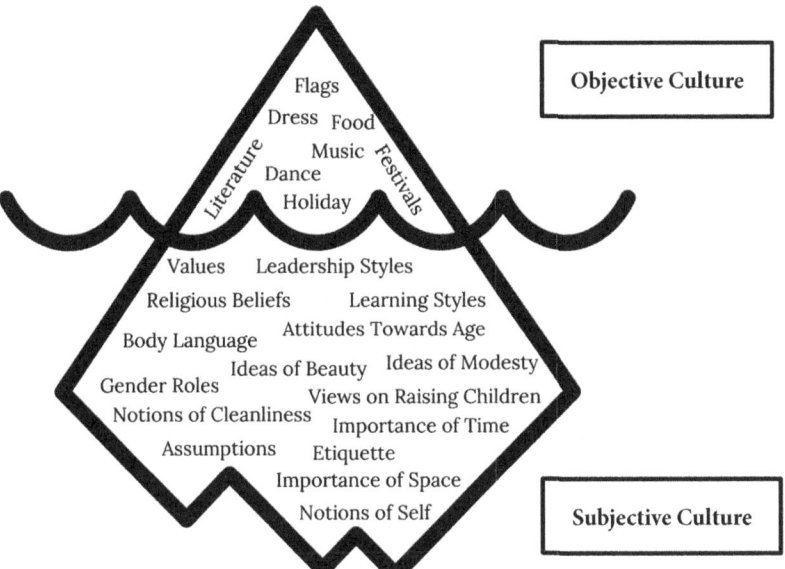

Ideas for Follow-Up

Watch a foreign movie and be alert to different aspects of subjective culture that differ from your own.

Study 6

Culture, Creation, and Fall

Open

The Creation, Fall, Redemption, Restoration view helps us have a gospel perspective on life, our world, and culture. How do these stages impact our relationships with God, ourselves, others, and the world?

Reflect on Scripture

Read these passages on Creation and complete the chart below.
God Creates Humankind: Gen. 1:26-31   Chosen in Him: Eph. 1:4-5

CREATION			
How we view SELF	How we view OTHERS	How we view GOD & the BIBLE	How we view THE WORLD

Re-read these passages on the Fall and complete the chart below.

No One Righteous: Rom. 3:10-12, 23
All Creation Affected: Rom. 8:22-23

IMPACT OF THE FALL			
How we view SELF	How we view OTHERS	How we view GOD & the BIBLE	How we view THE WORLD

Activity and Reflection

Dr. Kenneth Clark and Dr. Mamie Clark were African American psychologists known for their 1940s experiments using dolls to study children's attitudes about race. Their expert witness testimony became part of the 1954 Brown v. Board of Education Supreme Court ruling that found "separate but equal" segregation in public schools unconstitutional.

The Clarks showed children two identical dolls: a White doll and a Black doll. The experiments exposed the negative effects of racism and the internalized racist beliefs of the African American children. Social scientists are still reenacting the Clarks' doll experiment. Watch and then respond to the Clarks' doll experiment: https://www.youtube.com/watch?v=tkpUyB2xgTM.

- Did this contemporary reenactment surprise you? Why or why not?
- Why do you think the children answered this way?
- Where do the children get these messages?
- How does culture send these messages?

Study 7

Culture, Redemption, and Restoration

Open

In this lesson, we'll look at how Redemption and Restoration impact our relationships with God, ourselves, others, and the world.

Consider

1. As we grow in sanctification, we become more aware of God's holiness and our sinfulness. How does having a larger view of the cross help us bridge that gap?

2. Does the principle of simul justus et peccator (simultaneously justified and a sinner) turn your heart back to the gospel in gratitude? How does it help us not wallow in guilt?

Reflect on Scripture:
Read these passages and complete the chart below.

Redemption and Culture

Christ Redeemed Us: Gal. 3:13
A Redeemer: Rom. 3:23-25

IMPACT OF REDEMPTION			
How we view SELF	How we view OTHERS	How we view GOD & the BIBLE	How we view THE WORLD

Cultural misunderstandings, racism, and prejudice are a result of the Fall. Redemption begins our process of sanctification as the Holy Spirit shapes us.

How does redemption impact our ability to be united across race, culture, ethnicity, and other divisions? How does redemption impact our cultural intelligence?

Restoration and Culture

A New Heaven and Earth: Rev. 21:1-5
The Heavenly Jerusalem: Rev. 22:1-5

IMPACT OF RESTORATION			
How we view SELF	How we view OTHERS	How we view GOD & the BIBLE	How we view THE WORLD

"Jesus's vision for the climax of human history lauds the importance of ethnicity. (Rev. 7:9-20). ... It includes people from every nation, tribe, people, and language. ... At the end, we do not find the elimination of difference. Instead, the very diversity of cultures is a manifestation of God's glory."[1]

Ideas for Follow-Up

1. In your journal, or with a friend from the group, share a time when you found yourself stereotyping someone from a particular ethnic group, region, or occupation.

2. When did you see, experience, or become more aware of racial bias this past week? Either your own experience, someone else's, or in a news item?

Study 8

The Early Church Meets Culture

Open

How did the early church move from being a largely Jewish sect observing Jewish traditions to becoming a global, multicultural gospel movement?

Consider

How had God prepared the Jews to understand that his kingdom would embrace other nations as well? How had Jesus also shown this?

Reflect on Scripture
Read and respond to the following verses.

Phillip and Ethiopian: Acts 8:26-40

1. What does this passage show us about God's love for all nations?

2. In what ways was the Ethiopian an outsider?

The Overlooked Widows: Acts 6:1-7

1. What possible solutions might the apostles have considered? What were the benefits of appointing qualified leaders from among the Greek-speaking believers?

2. How might our churches "overlook widows"—believers who are different from us ethnically or culturally? Who might these people be? How could we address this wisely?

Peter and Cornelius: Acts 10

1. God needed to show Peter the vision three times for it to sink in. Why? What concepts were so hard for Peter to accept? Why might Luke have included multiple retellings in Acts 10 and 11?

2. How does Acts 10:28 dovetail with Ephesians 3:1-6? What is this "mystery" God has revealed?

Jesus, our perfect representative, fulfilled the Mosaic law, so Christians don't need to conform to ethnic Jewish life. God shows Peter that Jesus has broken down the dividing walls, uniting Jew and Gentile.

Ideas for Follow-Up

1. The apostles had to recognize their own cultural biases and deficiencies to ensure others were enfolded into the church and their needs met. Why is it helpful to think about our own culture as we consider our interactions with others from different cultures, backgrounds, races, or ethnicities?

Study 9

How Diversity Benefits the Church

Open

What blessings might we forgo when we fail to create an environment that welcomes others from different racial, ethnic, and economic groups?

Consider

What do you see as most beneficial about a diverse church? What aspects of diversity feel most challenging to you?

Reflect on Scripture
Read and respond to the following verses.

One Body, Many Parts: 1 Cor 12:12-27

1. How does Paul stress the unity of believers?

2. What do we learn about God in this passage? About people?

3. Paul writes that if one part of the body suffers, every part suffers with it. What would this look like in your church or community?

One in Christ: Eph. 2:11-22

Jews considered the divide between Jews and non-Jews (Gentiles) too wide to cross. Yet the Cross bridges this divide!

1. Paraphrase this passage in your own words.

2. What do we learn about the Father, the Son, and the Holy Spirit in this passage?

3. What do we learn about people?

> To picture the fully finished image of God you have to picture all of humanity unified in diversity under the lordship of Jesus Christ (Eph. 1:10; Col. 1:20) … in our role as prophets proclaiming God's truth to one another and the creation in our words and deeds; as priests continually dedicating all of ourselves to God in our words and deeds; as royalty exercising dominion over the creation in our care to the glory of God.[1] –Dr. Irwyn Ince, *The Beautiful Community*

Activity

The first step in growing in cross-cultural intelligence is to examine one's own culture. The following categories from *Resilient Ministry* identify several cultural domains that we may juggle regularly. Use this list to reflect on your own culture. Share your reflections with your group.

1. Personal—What expectations did your family have for you concerning education, sports, or social/political involvement?

2. Generational—What generational divisions do you see in your church?

3. Geography and demographics—What are some cultural

characteristics of your region?

4. Economic status—Have you ever felt conspicuously different in a social situation because of your income or lack of it?

5. Socioethnicity—Have you ever felt like you didn't belong because of your ethnicity or race?

Ideas for Follow-Up

1. What diversity exists in your community? A few internet clicks to research local census information might open your eyes to people groups you might not have noticed. Is my church reaching these people?

2. To learn more, read Chris Sick's short book, *Tangible: Making God known Through Deeds of Mercy and Words of Truth*.

Study 10

Race, Redemption, and the Multiethnic Church

Open

The Bible puts forth the goal and expectation of a unified church. Do most American churches reflect the diversity of their neighborhoods? How can churches create a welcoming environment for all?

Reflect on Scripture
Read and respond to the following verses.

One in Christ: Gal 3:26-29

In Galatians, Paul expounds on the "mystery" that Jews and Gentiles are united in the gospel. In this passage, he proclaims the unity and equality of several groups that were culturally and socially considered very unequal.

1. How did Jesus demonstrate this revolutionary principle in his ministry? Can you think of specific examples?

2. Does this passage mean we should we be colorblind? Does our identity in Christ cancel out our ethnic and gender identities? Why or why not? Can you think of Scriptures to support your answer?

Theologian Esau McCaulley, a professor at Wheaton College, points out the flaws in a "colorblind" theology. He writes that in this Galatians passage, Paul shows his "missional flexibility" as he relates to both Jewish and Gentile culture.

> The colorblind reading of Gal 3:28 is most flawed because it doesn't take the context of the book of Galatians seriously enough. The question that runs from one end of Galatians to the other is, Who are the rightful heirs to the promises made to Abraham. ... Paul's point is that being a Jew does not make you more of an heir to the promises in Christ than being a Gentile. It is a question about standing as it relates to the inheritance, not ethnic identity.[1]

The Mystery of Unity in Christ: Ephesians 3:2-9

1. What is the "mystery" Paul is privileged to teach and preach? What does the gospel accomplish for both Jews and Gentiles? (v. 6)

Discussion: Multicultural, Cross-Cultural, and Intercultural

Creating a multiethnic church is difficult. Dominant culture worshippers may struggle to adjust worship styles, music, etc. to accommodate other cultural expressions. People may believe their cultural preferences are a biblical imperative. It's easy to assume our background represents the biblical norm.

Discuss the following definitions from the Spring Institute.

What is the difference between multicultural, cross-cultural, and intercultural? While they all might be under the same roof, they describe entirely different rooms. The differences in the meanings have to do with the perspectives we take when interacting with people from other cultures.

Multicultural *refers to a society that contains several cultural or ethnic groups. People live alongside one another, but each cultural group does not necessarily have engaging interactions with each other. For example, in a multicultural neighborhood people may frequent ethnic grocery stores and restaurants without really interacting with their neighbors from other countries.*

Cross-cultural *deals with the comparison of different cultures. In cross-cultural communication, differences are understood and acknowledged, and can bring about individual change, but not collective transformations. In cross-cultural societies, one culture is often considered "the norm," and all other cultures are compared or contrasted to the dominant culture.*

Intercultural *describes communities in which there is a deep understanding and respect for all cultures. Intercultural communication focuses on the mutual exchange of ideas and cultural norms and the development of deep relationships.*

In an intercultural society, no one is left unchanged because everyone learns from one another and grows together.[2]

Discuss

- How do we know if something is a cultural preference or a biblical imperative in worship? For example, does the Bible speak to what music is appropriate? The level of physical movement? The use of prepared or extemporaneous prayers? How often should a church observe communion?

- Revisit the Readiness Skill in Study 2. How might this be helpful as we listen to others' perspectives in a multiethnic or intercultural church?

Ideas for Follow-Up

1. Watch this video clip of Martin Luther King Jr. on "Meet the Press," discussing the problem of church segregation in 1966. https://www.youtube.com/watch?v=1q881g1L_d8

2. Cultural Conversation Cards are a unique tool to encourage spiritual and cultural conversations about cultural values and experiences, family expectations, and ancestry. Find out more at www.culturalconversationcards.com

Study 11

The Miseducation of Maria Garriott

Open

Over half of the Bible is a history of God's dealing with humankind in both the Old and New Testaments. Why does God place such importance on knowing our history?

Consider

Why might this be helpful as we consider America's racial history?

Reflect on Scripture
Read and respond to the following verses.

Tell the Next Generation: Ps. 78:1-20
God calls us to think soberly about our collective history. This psalm rehearses the history of Israel, focusing on God's faithfulness and the misdeeds of his people.

1. List some of the specific examples of God's faithfulness.

2. List some of the specific examples of the people's unfaithfulness. How did God respond?

The Stoning of Stephen: Acts 7

1. Why did Stephen recite this long history of Israel—which his religious hearers already knew?

2. What does his hearers' response reveal about their hearts?

Discussion

1. What facts in this chapter about American history were new to you? How are you responding to this material?

2. Why is it important to examine the past in any discussion of racial and ethnic reconciliation?

Ideas for Follow-Up

1. Watch one of the "Race and the Church" videos online and be prepared to share a few points you learned from it. If you have time, write a journal response.

2. Watch a movie that explores some of American's racial history.

Study 12

Social Justice? Biblical Justice?

Open

Dr. Carl Ellis writes, "If we in the body of Christ let unbiblical understandings of 'social justice' prevail, then the social justice commanded by God in Scripture will remain unmet. Social justice is a biblical concept, and we must make a clear distinction between true social justice and today's distortions of it."[1]

Consider

The chapter listed many Bible passages showing God's command for justice, which are worth deeper study. What are some biblical principles of social justice?

Reflect on Scripture

The passages below are two examples of how God's people tried to survive and/or pursue justice during oppressive situations. Read and respond to the following passages.

Abraham, Sarah, and Pharaoh: Gen. 12:10-20

1. Why did Abraham ask Sarah to lie? What were Abraham's two bad choices in this passage?

2. Whom did God punish in this passage?

Theologian Carl Ellis says that "oppression is sin + power." Oppression is imposing your sin on someone else. "Oppression increases your proportion of bad options, decreases your proportion of good options. If 80% of my options are good, chances are that I'll choose a good option. But under oppression, 20% of options are good and the chance of choosing a good option decreases. Abraham had the choice of losing Sarah to Pharaoh and being killed or losing Sarah to Pharaoh and being paid."[2]

Ellis points out that God got angry at Pharaoh. Abraham repeated this behavior in Genesis 20, when he entered the land of Abimelek, king of Gerar. In both passages, the oppressive rulers are rebuked by God.

The Hebrew Midwives Disobey Pharaoh: Exodus 1:15-22

1. The Hebrews lived under the ethnicity-based slavery Pharaoh had instituted. What two bad choices did the Hebrew midwives Shiprah and Puah have?

2. Whom did God punish? Whom did God reward?

Determining what is righteous behavior is challenging under oppression. Some theologians believe the Hebrew midwives did not break the ninth commandment "Do not bear false witness against your neighbor." The purpose of the commandment is justice—protecting the reputation and possibly the life of another. The women disobeyed Pharaoh's command to commit infanticide to obey a higher law.

Discussion

It is often challenging to discern how to advocate for policies or laws that align with God's justice. For example, how should our country welcome the stranger or care for the poor? Discussions often break down along political lines. A conservative political worldview might say that poor people need to bear more personal responsibility and that people are poor because of their choices. A more liberal worldview would claim that the poverty is due to society's impact and systemic problems with schools, government, etc. How might these two worldviews look at the story of Abraham and Sarah?

Ideas for Follow-Up

1. Read and discuss Dr. Carl Ellis's article on the Gospel Coalition website, "Biblical Righteousness Is a Four-Paned Window." https://www.thegospelcoalition.org/article/biblical-righteousness-four-paned-window/

2. Read "Justice Too Long Delayed" on the *Christianity Today* website. Discuss it or write about it in your journal.

Study 13

Repenting and Lamenting

Open

The Bible tells us to "mourn with those who mourn" (Rom. 12:15). How do we demonstrate that empathy? How does the gospel enable us to enter into the suffering of others?

Consider

Why might people want to avoid lament and move quickly to fixing? Why is it beneficial to take the time to lament?

Reflect on Scripture
Read and respond to the following passages.

Nehemiah 1
Powerful empires desired Israel's trade routes, and the nation was conquered by the Assyrians (722 BCE) and the Babylonians, (586 BCE) who destroyed the temple and carried many Jews into exile. Some fifty years later, King Cyrus of Persia conquered the Babylonians and allowed Jews to return to Israel. Nehemiah has an important position with the Persian king in the capital city.

1. What did Nehemiah do first? What did lament look like?
2. What cultural, political, or personal obstacles did Nehemiah face in this chapter? How did he meet these challenges?

Psalm 79:8-9

1. What does the psalmist imply about past sins in these verses?

2. What reason does the psalmist give as to why God should help him and his people?

Dan. 9:1-19

Daniel reads from the prophecies of Jeremiah about the destruction of Jerusalem (Jer. 25, 29) and pleads for God's mercy.

1. What does Daniel ask God's forgiveness for?

2. What is Daniel's attitude as he approaches God?

Ideas for Action

1. According to author and professor Brené Brown, shame says "you are bad," while guilt says "you did a bad thing." Shame can lead to a spiral of paralysis and self-hate. Guilt, on the other hand, can motivate positive change. Why is this a significant distinction in the discussion of racial healing? What might lament look like for us?

2. Rev. Eric Mason, founder and pastor of Epiphany Fellowship Church in Philadelphia, says, "Our culture teaches us to 'just get over' pain. Lamenting allows us to enter it. It is emotionally healthy to enter into grief. It's also biblical.... [Lament] has historically been an important part of the black church.... To experience real change, we must learn to lament together."[1] Do you agree or disagree? Has lament been part of your church experience? Write your response.

Study 14

Privileges and Rights

Open

People of color in the U.S. have not enjoyed the same validation and economic and physical security as those of European descent, in both explicit and implicit ways. Do you agree or disagree with this statement?

Consider

After reading the chapter, what privileges do you see God has given you?

Reflect on Scripture

Paul's Privileged Background: Phil. 3:4-6

1. How does Paul describe himself here? What privileges did he enjoy because of his background and position?

2. Did he value his background? In what way?

Paul Renounces His Rights: 1 Cor. 9:15-27
In 1 Corinthians 9, Paul lists some of the rights he has not claimed (including the right of financial support) because he doesn't want to create any obstacles to the gospel.

1. What intentional choices has Paul made?

2. How might you apply these verses to the concept of rights or privilege in our culture?

3. What privileges do you enjoy? List them. Consider your race, age, health, education, attractiveness, ability or disability level, natural talents, and skills. In what ways would you say, "I pulled myself up with my bootstraps," and in what ways would you say, "I had very little to do with this advantage."

Rev. Randy Nabors, who planted and pastored New City Fellowship in Chattanooga, Tennessee for 36 years and founded a network of multiethnic churches, points to 1 Cor. 9 as a biblical strategy for cross-cultural ministry.

> Crossing cultures for the sake of Christ and to win others to Christ is an intentional process of becoming a "slave" to that people group. It is not becoming a casual and distant observer, nor a tourist, and not even a cultural anthropologist, but a slave…Loving your neighbor as yourself can be more complicated in a multiethnic and multicultural environment… Crossing cultures is a process of becoming …. It is an intentional, purposeful, and dedicated pursuit of listening to, learning from, engaging with, and feeling the pain, aspirations, hopes, and dreams of another culture.[1]

Ideas for Follow-Up

1. Professor George Yancey, author of *Beyond Racial Gridlock: Embracing Mutual Responsibility* (IVP, 2006) points out that Christianity offers a unique approach to issues of race relations compared to the secular ideologies of our day. Watch his presentation on The Gospel Coalition website. https://

www.thegospelcoalition.org/blogs/justin-taylor/a-christian-approach-to-moving-beyond-racial-gridlock-an-alternative-to-secular-black-lives-matter-and-all- lives-matter-ideologies/

2. Ken Sande, the author of *Peacemakers* and *Relational Wisdom*, published "What You Can Do About Racial Tensions" on his website. It includes a video, "Black Parents Explain How to Deal with the Police." Watch this video and discuss it. https://rw360.org/2020/06/03/what-you-can-do-about-racial-tensions/

Study 15

Repairing What is Broken

Open

The Bible explains both the inherent value and sinful tendencies of humankind. We exhibit dignity and depravity, both individually and collectively, and the structures and systems we create reflect that. Yet God uses his people to participate in his movement of healing and restoration through word and deed.

Consider

How does having greater cross-cultural understanding impact the way we partner with God in his restoration process?

Reflect on Scripture

The Good Samaritan: Luke 10:25-37

Isaiah 58:1-10

Jesus's first sermon, which we studied in Lesson 3 (Luke 4:16-22), alludes to several passages in Isaiah, including these verses from chapter 58.

1. What do these verses reveal about God's desire?

2. What do these verses reveal about people?

3. Are there practical ways we can obey these verses?

Rev. Esau McCaulley says that Jesus quotes these verses to denounce "fake religiosity more concerned with ritual than transforming the lived situation of the poor. According to Isaiah, true practice of religion ought to result in concrete change, the breaking of yokes. He does not mean the occasional private act of liberation, but 'to break the chains of injustice.' What could this mean other than a transformation of the structures of societies that trap people in hopelessness? Jesus has in mind the creation of a different type of world."[1]

Ideas for Follow-Up

1. Phil Vischer, the creator of Veggie Tales, records "Holy Post" podcasts providing a Christian view of contemporary issues. Watch his "Race in America" post on YouTube. https://www.youtube.com/watch?v=AGUwcs9qJXY

2. The Intercultural Development Inventory (IDI) is a useful tool to assess one's cultural intelligence, or the ability to function effectively across various cultural contexts. The IDI is used by denominations, universities, businesses, and individuals to help leaders explore their orientation and thinking patterns when relating to people from cultures that are different from their own. Learn more at the Christian Cultural Intelligence Group https://www.developingculturalintelligence.com/

Study 16

Hospitality

Open

How can we create a welcoming environment for all? Share or write about a time you felt welcome and included into a community.

Consider

What comes to mind when you hear the word "hospitality"? Does your image line up with biblical hospitality?

Reflect on Scripture

Hospitality in the Early Church: Acts 2:42-47

1. The early church united Jew and Gentile, slave and free, male and female, rich and poor. How do you see that unity demonstrated in practical hospitality here?

2. How did the world respond to this radical hospitality and unity?

The Sheep and the Goats: Matt. 25:31-46

1. What does this passage say about what God values?

2. What emotions do you feel reading this passage?

Ideas for Follow-Up

1. Darryl Davis, a respected Black musician, befriended members of the KKK. How did his practice of hospitality disarm an enemy? Watch and respond to his TEDTalk on YouTube. https://www.youtube.com/watch?v=Y4gly9n9RBo

2. Artist and designer Yang Liu was born in China but has lived in Germany since she was 14. She compares the differences between the two cultures in a series of images. View and discuss her images at http://bsix12.com/east-meets-west/

Study 17

A Harder Bridge to Cross

Open

In this lesson, we'll discover what the Bible teaches about caring for those who are materially disadvantaged, and learn a tool to help cross the socio-economic divide.

Consider

What obstacles do you face when interacting with people who are either much wealthier or poorer than you?

Reflect on Scripture

Store our treasures in Heaven: Matt. 6:19-24

Jesus assumes that his followers will give to the needy, and urges them not to call attention to themselves when doing so. He tells us how we deal with our treasure reveals our hearts.

1. What does this passage teach about God?

2. What does this passage teach about people?

3. How can I obey this passage in practical ways?

Faith Without Works is Dead: James 2:1-14
1. James, the brother of Jesus, writes believers to urge them to be "doers of the Word." (1:22) What does this passage say about what God values?

2. What does this passage say about what people tend to value?

Ideas for Follow Up

1. The following resources would be especially helpful in guiding Christian engagement with the materially poor: *When Helping Hurts*, by Fikkert & Corbett; *Toxic Charity*, by Bob Lupton; and *Merciful: The Opportunity and Challenge of Discipling the Poor out of Poverty* by Randy Nabors.

2. Watch and discuss this video "Grace, Justice and Mercy" of a discussion between Rev. Tim Keller and Bryan Stevenson, whose book *Just Mercy* chronicles his nonprofit work to bring legal justice to the poor and the incarcerated. Stevenson sees his work as a logical extension of his faith. "To me, the Great Commission is a call to get proximate—to the places in our nation, in our world, where there's suffering and abuse and neglect." He admits that "If you do uncomfortable things, it will break you. But in brokenness, we are filled with grace and mercy." https://www.hfny.org/blog/what-we-learned-tim-keller-bryan-stevenson-last-week

Study 18

Partnering with God in Restoration

Open

The author writes, "God is reweaving the torn fabric of society through his people, the church." How does God use us in this process?

Consider

How does growing in ability to relate across cultures, ethnicities and races help us be better witnesses?

Reflect on Scripture

Zacchaeus Meets Jesus: Luke 19:1-10

To fellow Jews, Zacchaeus was a traitor; to the Romans, a tool. He collaborated with the Roman occupiers to collect burdensome taxes. Tax collectors also enriched themselves by extorting additional fees. So imagine the scandal, grumbling, and resentment of the crowd when Rabbi Jesus selected this taxman to host a welcome dinner.

1. What do we learn about Jesus in this passage?

2. If Zacchaeus's identity had previously been tied to his wealth, what does his response demonstrate?

3. In *Christianity Today,* editor Timothy Dalrymple writes, "Zacchaeus had not personally designed the unjust system of Roman taxation. But …he had participated in it and profited from it… Zacchaeus did not merely repent of his ways; he made restitution. He set up what we might call a 'Zacchaeus fund' in order to restore what belonged to his neighbors." Do you agree that righteousness has practical expressions in justice? What might this look like today?

True Justice: Micah 6:8

In Micah 6, God condemns the violence and injustice he sees among his people. He says that true repentance, and true worship is accompanied by a godly life.

1. Paraphrase this verse. What is the true justice God requires?

2. How does this verse agree with other passages we have studied?

For Follow Up

Read and discuss the following article, which uses the mnemonic SCHOLAR to summarize the concepts in this study. Share with others how you might implement some of what you've learned.

Be a SCHOLAR

Cultural intelligence is fluid. We can always grow, and we need to keep growing because the culture around us continues to change. As we respond to the challenges of our culture, we contextualize but don't compromise the gospel.

The following mnemonic device can help you remember some of the main points of these lessons on unity and growing in your ability to cross cultures effectively. Keep learning, listening, reflecting, and practicing!

Study God's Word and his plan for unity in diversity and his plan to redeem all ethnos (people groups) as revealed in Scripture. Our primary identity is in Christ; we are a new humanity, not just a new individual.

Confess- ask God to reveal how self-love and pride blocks our love of others who are different from us. Confess, and experience forgiveness. Have a humble, teachable attitude of gentleness and empathy; recognize your own cultural preferences as one way of looking at the world. Recognize that some of our ways of living are not in line with Biblical principles. Recognize our desire for the personal comfort and security of our own cultural context.

Have new experiences - Be intentional and curious! Place yourself in a different cultural setting – an ethnic restaurant, or a worship service from a different tradition. Reach out to other races and ethnic groups; listen to their stories and concerns. Ask what they see as strengths or assets of their culture or ethnicity. Befriend a minority family in your neighborhood, not as a project, but as people. Ask good questions (but be aware that many cultures consider direct "why" questions rude; do your homework first, and have cultural informants/ teachers).

> **Open up to a covenantal gospel**- Recognize and confess corporate responsibility for national and church sins of racism as Daniel and Nehemiah did (see Dan. 9:1-19 and Neh. 1:4-7). Acknowledge and fight systemic injustices.
>
> **Learn** from and be ministered to by people different from you; learn about other people groups, their histories and backgrounds. Read books or watch movies about different cultures/experiences. Listen to the experiences of others.
>
> **Anticipate hardships.** Cross-cultural experiences create disequilibrium because they take us out of our culture zone, but they have a high potential for learning. Accept failure as part of the process.
>
> **Reflect**- Become aware of the invisible influence of culture in our lives. Stop and consider what you're thinking, feeling, doing. Write in a journal, identify your cultural rules and preferences and their influences, and debrief with others.

Reflect

1. What are some of your key takeaways from this study?

2. What are some tangible steps you can take to implement this learning?

Ideas for Follow Up

1. Because we often have such dramatically different lived experiences, we must listen to one another's stories. This is especially true in cross-cultural relationships. A Story Feast, as outlined by Elizabeth Turnage, is an intentional gathering with others to share our stories. For ideas on how to do this, visit https://encourage.pcacdm.org/wp-content/uploads/2018/09/StoryFeastHandout18.pdf

2. For additional ideas for follow up, visit the author's book page www.strongertogethergospel.com.

ACKNOWLEDGEMENTS

Sir Winston Churchill said, "Writing a book is an adventure. To begin with it is a toy and an amusement. Then it becomes a mistress, then it becomes a master, then it becomes a tyrant. The last phase is that just as you are about to be reconciled to your servitude, you kill the monster and fling him to the public." This book is an imperfect offering into an important, complicated, and ongoing discussion.

The handprints of Parakaleo, a ministry I've been part of since 2009, are all over this book, and I taught some of this material in online cohorts in 2017. I'm grateful for how Parakaleo helps me and other pastoral spouses keep the gospel at the center of our hearts.

The encouragement of my friend Rev. Wy Plummer, who leads the PCA's African American Ministries, has been pivotal to helping me believe a middle-aged White lady might have something to add to the discussion on unity and race.

Pam Grabe, Ann Maouyo, Denine Blevins, and Donna Sauter waded into messy first drafts and saved me from a multitude of errors. Kim Sutter and Alison Currie also provided valuable feedback. Julie Serven's excellent copyediting corrected numerous errors.

Margaret Osburn and the Deepdene Writers critiqued the essays in this book, and the input of such a talented, diverse group of writers has been a gift. I'm still learning from you all.

My in-laws, Pete and Cleo Garriott, have demonstrated unflagging grace ever since I joined their family. I am grateful for my beloved children, who allowed me to tell some of their stories here. Finally, my husband Craig has articulated and modeled the gospel and its application to ethic unity to me for over forty years. He read multiple drafts, and helped me hone closer to theological clarity and balance. I love him dearly.

ABOUT THE AUTHOR

Maria Garriott and her husband Craig planted Faith Christian Fellowship, an urban multiethnic, socio-economically diverse church in Baltimore, where they served for 38 years. In 2018, they founded Baltimore Antioch Leadership Movement (BALM), a ministry to multiply cross-cultural disciple-making leaders. Maria is a coach and network leader for Parakaleo, a global ministry to church planting women. She received a M.S. in Professional Writing and wrote curricula for The Johns Hopkins University School of Education for 20 years. She has published numerous articles, essays, and poems, as well as a memoir of urban church planting, *A Thousand Resurrections*. Maria and Craig have five adult children and seven grandchildren.

BIBLIOGRAPHY

"A Brief History of Jim Crow." Constitutional Rights Foundation. Accessed June 11, 2021. https://www.crf-usa.org/black-history-month/a-brief-history-of-jim-crow.

"American Indian Boarding Schools." Wikipedia. Wikimedia Foundation, June 13, 2021. https://en.wikipedia.org/wiki/American_Indian_boarding_schools.

"Asian Americans Are the Least Likely Group in the U.S. to Be Promoted to Management." Harvard Business Review, May 31, 2018. https://hbr.org/2018/05/asian-americans-are-the-least-likely-group-in-the-u-s-to-be-promoted-to-management.

"Bartolomé De Las Casas." Wikipedia. Wikimedia Foundation, July 30, 2021. https://en.wikipedia.org/wiki/Bartolom%C3%A9_de_las_Casas.

"Carlisle Indian School Digital Resource Center." "Kill the Indian in him, and save the man": R. H. Pratt on the Education of Native Americans | Carlisle Indian School Digital Resource Center. Accessed August 3, 2021. http://carlisleindian.dickinson.edu/teach/kill-indian-him-and-save-man-r-h-pratt-education-native-americans.

"Chinese Immigration | History Detectives." PBS. Public Broadcasting Service. Accessed June 17, 2021. https://www.pbs.org/opb/historydetectives/feature/chinese-immigration/.

"Criminal Justice Facts." The Sentencing Project, June 3, 2021. https://www.sentencingproject.org/criminal-justice-facts/.

"Divided by Faith?" ChristianityToday.com. Christianity Today, October 2, 2000. https://www.christianitytoday.com/ct/2000/october2/1.34.html.

"Economic Issues 10 -- Deindustrialization -- Its Causes and Implications." International Monetary Fund. Accessed June 17, 2021. https://www.imf.org/EXTERNAL/PUBS/FT/ISSUES10/INDEX.HTM.

"Genetic Impact of African Slave Trade Revealed in DNA Study." BBC News. BBC, July 24, 2020. https://www.bbc.com/news/world-africa-53527405.

"Georgetown Reflects on Slavery, Memory, and Reconciliation." Georgetown University, May 26, 2021. http://slavery.georgetown.edu/.

"Guns Germs & Steel: Variables. Smallpox." PBS. Public Broadcasting Service. Accessed June 17, 2021. https://www.pbs.org/gunsgermssteel/variables/smallpox.html.

"History of Native Americans in the United States." Wikipedia. Wikimedia Foundation, June 3, 2021. https://en.wikipedia.org/wiki/History_of_Native_Americans_in_the_United_States.

"In U.S., Decline of Christianity Continues at Rapid Pace." Pew Research Center's Religion & Public Life Project, June 9, 2020. https://www.pewforum.org/2019/10/17/in-u-s-decline-of-christianity-continues-at-rapid-pace/.

"James Baldwin." Oxford Reference. Accessed June 17, 2021. https://www.oxfordreference.com/view/10.1093/acref/9780191843730.001.0001/q-oro-ed5-00000730.

"John Brown." American Battlefield Trust. Accessed August 4, 2021. https://www.battlefields.org/learn/biographies/john-brown?ms=googlegrant&gclid=CjwKCAjw9aiIBhA1EiwAJ_GTStz1ry6-rpU_eLdgcUmy26vBX80AIG2SNtG87mK-IAVoAvBkioUYEBoC0CMQAvD_BwE.

"K-12 Disparity Facts and Statistics." UNCF. UNCF , March 20, 2020. https://uncf.org/pages/k-12-disparity-facts-and-stats.

"Mass Incarceration." American Civil Liberties Union. Accessed August 3, 2021. https://www.aclu.org/issues/smart-justice/mass-incarceration.

"Race - The Power of an Illusion. Go Deeper." PBS. Public Broadcasting Service. Accessed June 17, 2021. https://www.pbs.org/race/000_About/002_06-godeeper.htm.

"Racial and Ethnic Disparities Continue in Pregnancy-Related Deaths." Centers for Disease Control and Prevention. Centers for Disease Control and Prevention, September 6, 2019. https://www.cdc.gov/media/releases/2019/p0905-racial-ethnic-disparities-pregnancy-deaths.html.

"Slavery in Portugal." Wikipedia. Wikimedia Foundation, June 1, 2021. https://en.wikipedia.org/wiki/Slavery_in_Portugal.

"Slavery, United States." Slavery, United States - Places in History (Library of Congress). Accessed June 9, 2021. https://www.loc.gov/rr/geogmap/placesinhistory/archive/2011/20110318_slavery.html.

"Sunday Morning in America Still Segregated – and That's Ok With Worshippers." Lifeway Research, December 22, 2020. https://lifewayresearch.com/2015/01/15/sunday-morning-in-america-still-segregated-and-thats-ok-with-worshipers/.

"The Church of Individualism - Mere Orthodoxy: Christianity, Politics, and Culture." Mere Orthodoxy | Christianity, Politics, and Culture, September 8, 2020. https://mereorthodoxy.com/the-church-of-individualism/.

"The King Philosophy - Nonviolence365®." The King Center, January 5, 2021. https://thekingcenter.org/about-tkc/the-king-philosophy/.

"The Westminster Larger Catechism (1648) by Westminster Divines." Ligonier Ministries. Accessed June 16, 2021. https://www.ligonier.org/learn/articles/westminster-larger-catechism/.

"White Christians Have Become Even Less Motivated to Address Racial Injustice." Barna Group. Accessed June 9, 2021. https://www.barna.com/research/american-christians-race-problem/.

"White Supremacy." Merriam-Webster. Merriam-Webster. Accessed June 23, 2021. https://www.merriam-webster.com/dictionary/white%20supremacy.

"Yellow Peril." Wikipedia. Wikimedia Foundation, June 12, 2021. https://en.wikipedia.org/wiki/Yellow_Peril#Literary_Yellow_Peril.

Alexander, Michelle. The New Jim Crow: Mass Incarceration in the Age of Colorblindness. New York: New Press, 2020.

Anyabwile, Thabiti. "Learning to Be the Moral Minority from a Moral Minority." The Gospel Coalition, February 4, 2013. https://www.thegospelcoalition.org/blogs/thabiti-anyabwile/learning-to-be-the-moral-minority-from-a-moral-minority.

Arana, Marie. "Perspective | A History of Anti-Hispanic Bigotry in the United States." The Washington Post. WP Company, August 9, 2019. https://www.washingtonpost.com/outlook/a-

history-of-anti-hispanic-bigotry-in-the-united-states/
2019/08/09/5ceaacba-b9f2-11e9-b3b4-2bb69e8c4e39_story.html.

Baptist, Edward E. Half Has Never Been Told: Slavery and the Making of American Capitalism. New York: Basic Books, 2016.

Batalova , Jeanne, and Mary Hanna. "Frequently Requested Statistics on Immigrants and Immigration in the United States." migrationpolicy.org, May 14, 2021. https://www.migrationpolicy.org/article/frequently-requested-statistics-immigrants-and-immigration-united-states-2020.

Bear, Charla. "American Indian Boarding Schools Haunt Many." NPR. NPR, May 12, 2008. https://www.npr.org/templates/story/story.php?storyId=16516865#:~:text=The%20federal%20government%20began%20sending,developed%20in%20an%20Indian%20prison.

Beck, John A. Basic Bible Atlas. Grand Rapids, MI: Baker Book House, 2020.

Beyond Diversity: What the Future of Racial Justice Will Require of U.S. Churches. Barna Group, 2021.

Bradley, Anthony. "Critical Race Theory Isn't a Threat for Presbyterians." Mere Orthodoxy | Christianity, Politics, and Culture, February 3, 2021. https://mereorthodoxy.com/critical-race-theory-presbyterian-church-in-america/.

Bureau, US Census. "Hispanic Heritage Month 2020." The United States Census Bureau, September 22, 2020. https://www.census.gov/newsroom/facts-for-features/2020/hispanic-heritage-month.html.

Bureau, US Census. "Hispanic Heritage Month 2020." The United States Census Bureau, September 22, 2020. https://

www.census.gov/newsroom/facts-for-features/2020/hispanic-heritage-month.html.

Burns, Bob, Tasha Chapman, and Donald Guthrie. Resilient Ministry: What Pastors Told Us about Surviving and Thriving. Downers Grove, IL: IVP Books, 2013.

Campbell, Adina. "What Is Black Lives Matter and What Are the Aims?" BBC News. BBC, June 12, 2021. https://www.bbc.com/news/explainers-53337780.

Cartagena, Nathan Luis. "What Christians Get Wrong About Critical Race Theory – Part II." Accessed June 12, 2021. Faithfully Magazine, December 29, 2020. https://faithfullymagazine.com/critical-race-theory-christians-two/.

Cartagena, Nathan. "What Christians Get Wrong About Critical Race Theory – Part I." Accessed June 1, 2021. Faithfully Magazine, December 29, 2020. https://faithfullymagazine.com/critical-race-theory-christians/.

Cox, Daniel, and Robert P. Jones. "America's Changing Religious Identity." PRRI. Accessed June 1, 2021. https://www.prri.org/research/american-religious-landscape-christian-religiously-unaffiliated/.

Dalrymple, Timothy. "Justice Too Long Delayed." ChristianityToday.com. Christianity Today, June 10, 2020. https://www.christianitytoday.com/ct/2020/june-web-only/justice-too-long-delayed.html.

Desmond, Matthew. "American Capitalism Is Brutal. You Can Trace That to the Plantation." Accessed June 12, 2021. The New York Times. The New York Times, August 14, 2019. https://www.nytimes.com/interactive/2019/08/14/magazine/slavery-capitalism.html.

DiAngelo, Robin J., and Alex Tatusian. White Fragility. New York, NY: Public Science, 2016.

Douglass, Frederick. Narrative of the Life of Frederick Douglass, an American Slave and Other Writings. New York: Fall River Press, 2012.

Duson, Monique. "Do the 'Work.'" CFBU, June 5, 2020. https://www.centerforbiblicalunity.com/post/do-the-work.

Duson, Monique. "Reparations: Justice or Theft?" CFBU, June 11, 2020. https://www.centerforbiblicalunity.com/post/reparations-justice-or-theft.

Duson, Monique. "The Father, Son, & Antiracism." CFBU, January 19, 2021. https://www.centerforbiblicalunity.com/post/the-father-son-antiracism.

Duson, Monique. "The Myth of Reverse Racism." CFBU, August 15, 2020. https://www.centerforbiblicalunity.com/post/the-myth-of-reverse-racism.

Dykstra-Pruim, Pennylyn. Understanding Us & Them: Interpersonal Cultural Intelligence for Community Building. Grand Rapids, MI: The Calvin Press, 2019.

Edelman, Richard. "Our America: A Hispanic History of the United States." Edelman. Accessed June 12, 2021. https://www.edelman.com/insights/our-america-hispanic-history-united-states.

Edwards, Frank, Hedwig Lee, and Michael Esposito. "Risk of Being Killed by Police Use of Force in the United States by Age, Race–Ethnicity, and Sex." Accessed May 4, 2021. PNAS. National Academy of Sciences, August 20, 2019. https://www.pnas.org/content/116/34/16793.

Edwards, Korie Little. "The Multiethnic Church Movement Hasn't Lived up to Its Promise." Accessed June 20, 2021. ChristianityToday.com. Christianity Today, February 16, 2021. https://www.christianitytoday.com/ct/2021/march/race-diversity-multiethnic-church-movement-promise.html.

Ellis, Carl, and Carl Ellis. "Biblical Perspectives on Race." Potomac Presbytery Retreat. Lecture presented at the Potomac Presbytery Retreat, September 18, 2018.

Ellis, Carl. "Biblical Righteousness Is a Four-Paned Window." The Gospel Coalition, August 22, 2018. https://www.thegospelcoalition.org/article/biblical-righteousness-four-paned-window/.

Emerson, Michael O., and Christian Smith. Divided by Faith: Evangelical Religion and the Problem of Race in America. Oxford, NY: Oxford University Press, 2000.

Freeman, James. "Opinion | Black Lives Matter and the Family." The Wall Street Journal. Dow Jones & Company, July 23, 2020. https://www.wsj.com/articles/black-lives-matter-and-the-family-11595530123.

French, David. "When Our Forefathers Fail." The French Press. The Dispatch, May 30, 2021. https://frenchpress.thedispatch.com/p/when-our-forefathers-fail.

Frey, William H. "The US Will Become 'Minority White' in 2045, Census Projects." Brookings. Brookings, September 10, 2018. https://www.brookings.edu/blog/the-avenue/2018/03/14/the-us-will-become-minority-white-in-2045-census-projects/.

Hamren, Kelly, Ed Stetzer, and Sadiri Joy Tira. "Social Justice, Critical Race Theory, Marxism, and Biblical Ethics." The Exchange | A Blog by Ed Stetzer. Accessed June 17, 2021. https://

www.christianitytoday.com/edstetzer/2020/june/reflections-from-christian-scholar-on-social-justice-critic.html.

Harris, John. The Last Slave Ships: New York and the End of the Middle Passage. Boston, MA: Yale University Press, 2022.

Hayoun, Massoud. "Japanese Americans' Fight for Post-Internment Reparations Offers a Blueprint for Tackling Inequality in the Trump Era.". Pacific Standard, August 1, 2018. https://psmag.com/social-justice/japanese-americans-fight-for-post-internment-reparations-offers-a-blueprint-for-fighting-inequality-in-the-trump-era.

Hill, Daniel. White Awake: an Honest Look at What It Means to Be White. Downers Grove, IL: InterVarsity Press, 2017.

History.com Editors. "Hispanic History Milestones: Timeline." History.com. A&E Television Networks, September 14, 2020. https://www.history.com/topics/hispanic-history/hispanic-latinx-milestones.

History.com Editors. "Hispanic History Milestones: Timeline." History.com. A&E Television Networks, September 14, 2020. https://www.history.com/topics/hispanic-history/hispanic-latinx-milestones.

History.com Editors. "The Red Summer of 1919." History.com. A&E Television Networks, December 2, 2009. https://www.history.com/topics/black-history/chicago-race-riot-of-1919.

History.com Editors. "Tulsa Race Massacre." History.com. A&E Television Networks, March 8, 2018. https://www.history.com/topics/roaring-twenties/tulsa-race-massacre.

Hochschild, Adam. Bury the Chains: Prophets and Rebels in the Fight to Free an Empire's Slaves. Boston: Houghton Mifflin, 2006.

Holy Bible: English Standard Version. Wheaton, IL: Crossway Bibles, 2001.

Ince, Irwyn L. The Beautiful Community: Unity, Diversity, and the Church at Its Best. Downers Grove, IL: InterVarsity Press, 2020.

Johnson , Ben. "What Does 'Black Lives Matter' Believe?" Acton Institute PowerBlog, August 14, 2020. https://blog.acton.org/archives/116471-explainer-what-does-black-lives-matter-believe.html?utm_term=black+lives+matter+political+organization&utm_campaign=Blog%2BPosts&utm_source=adwords&utm_medium=ppc&hsa_acc=9098040689&hsa_cam=13422215022&hsa_grp=106229721498&hsa_ad=450115522526&hsa_src=g&hsa_tgt=kwd-926975091586&hsa_kw=black+lives+matter+political+organization&hsa_mt=b&hsa_net=adwords&hsa_ver=3&gclid=CjwKCAjwwqaGBhBKEiwAMk-FtFrUxY73aRFTTuF7hIEHu-1zLrWYgpd6UgJsYbsy4-5woeuMJ6d-VRoCsTEQAvD_BwE.

Katznelson, Ira. When Affirmative Action Was White: an Untold History of Racial Inequality in Twentieth-Century America. New York: W.W. Norton, 2006.

Keller, Tim. "The Bible and Race." Life in the Gospel, September 30, 2020. https://quarterly.gospelinlife.com/the-bible-and-race/.

Keller, Timothy. "A Biblical Critique of Secular Justice and Critical Theory." Life in the Gospel, September 30, 2020. https://quarterly.gospelinlife.com/a-biblical-critique-of-secular-justice-and-critical-theory/.

Kwon, Duke L., and Gregory Thompson. Reparations: A Christian Call for Repentance and Repair. Grand Rapids, MI: Brazos Press, a division of Baker Publishing Group, 2021.

Layton, Aaron J. Dear White Christian: What Every White Christian Needs to Know about How Black Christians See, Think & Experience Racism in America: Respectfully Written by a Black Christian. Lawrenceville, GA: Committee on Discipleship Ministries, 2017.

Livermore, David A. Cultural Intelligence: Improving Your CQ to Engage Our Multicultural World. Baker Academic: Grand Rapids, MI, 2009.

Loritts, Bryan C. Insider Outsider: My Journey as a Stranger in White Evangelicalism and My Hope for Us All. Grand Rapids, MI: Zondervan, 2018.

Martí, Gerardo, and Mark Mulder. "More than a Fiesta -- Variety and Diversity among Latino Protestants in the U.S." Faith and Leadership. Duke University, September 18, 2018. https://faithandleadership.com/gerardo-marti-and-mark-t-mulder-more-fiesta-variety-and-diversity-among-latino-protestants-us.

Mason, Eric. Woke Church: an Urgent Call for Christians in America to Confront Racism and Injustice. Chicago, IL: Moody Publishers, 2018.

Mathison, Keith. "All Truth Is God's Truth - A Reformed Approach to Science and Scripture." Ligonier Ministries. Accessed June 17, 2021. https://www.ligonier.org/blog/all-truth-gods-truth-reformed-approach-science-and-scripture/.

McCaulley, Esau. Reading While Black. Downers Grove, IL: InterVarsity Press, 2020.

McIntosh, Peggy. "White Privilege: Unpacking the Invisible Knapsack." UMBC Psychology Department. orig. published in Peace and Freedom magazine, July/Aug. 1989, n.d. https://psychology.umbc.edu/files/2016/10/White-

Privilege_McIntosh-1989.pdf.

McWhorter, John. "The Dehumanizing Condescension of 'White Fragility'." The Atlantic. Atlantic Media Company, July 15, 2020. https://www.theatlantic.com/ideas/archive/2020/07/dehumanizing-condescension-white-fragility/614146/.

Mez, Kristin Du. "#Leave LOUD and the Evangelical Reckoning." Anxious Bench. Patheos, March 18, 2021. https://www.patheos.com/blogs/anxiousbench/2021/03/leaveloud-and-the-evangelical-reckoning/.

Murray, David P. Essay. In The Happy Christian: Ten Ways to Be a Joyful Believer in a Gloomy World. Nashville, TN: Nelson Books, 2015.

Nabors, Randy. Insufficient: Pursuing Grace-Based Pastoral Competence . White Blackbird Books, 2020.

Newbell, Trillia J. United: Captured by God's Vision for Diversity. Chicago, IL: Moody Publishers, 2014.

Ortiz, V, and E Telles. "Racial Identity and Racial Treatment of Mexican Americans." Race and social problems. U.S. National Library of Medicine. Accessed June 16, 2021. https://pubmed.ncbi.nlm.nih.gov/24307918/.

Parker, Kim, and Ruth Igielnik. "What We Know About Gen Z So Far." Pew Research Center's Social & Demographic Trends Project. Pew Research Center. Accessed May 31, 2021. https://www.pewresearch.org/social-trends/2020/05/14/on-the-cusp-of-adulthood-and-facing-an-uncertain-future-what-we-know-about-gen-z-so-far-2/.

Parker, Kim, Juliana Menasce Horowitz, and Monica Anderson. "Majorities Across Racial, Ethnic Groups Express Support for the

Black Lives Matter Movement." Pew Research Center's Social & Demographic Trends Project. Pew Research Center, December 17, 2020. https://www.pewresearch.org/social-trends/2020/06/12/amid-protests-majorities-across-racial-and-ethnic-groups-express-support-for-the-black-lives-matter-movement/.

Passel, Jeffrey S., and D'Vera Cohn. "U.S. Population Projections: 2005-2050." Pew Research Center's Hispanic Trends Project. Pew Research Center, May 30, 2020. https://www.pewresearch.org/hispanic/2008/02/11/us-population-projections-2005-2050/.

Pei, Adrian. The Minority Experience: Navigating Emotional and Organizational Realities. Downers Grove, IL, IL: IVP Books, an imprint of InterVarsity Press, 2018.

Pitts, Leonard. "'I'm Not a Racist' Is Not a Good Defense for Racist Behavior." www.baltimoresun.com . The Baltimore Sun, June 15, 2020.

Pohl, Christine D. Essay. In Living into Community: Cultivating Practices That Sustain Us, 2. Grand Rapids, MI: William B. Eerdmans Publishing Company, 2012.

Rah, Soong-Chan. Essay. In Prophetic Lament: a Call for Justice in Troubled Times, 64–65, 68. InterVarsity Press, 2015.

Robertson, Campbell. "A Quiet Exodus: Why Black Worshipers Are Leaving White Evangelical Churches." The New York Times, March 9, 2018. https://www.nytimes.com/2018/03/09/us/blacks-evangelical-churches.html.

Rudolph, Dana. "White Privilege: Unpacking the Invisible Knapsack' and 'Some Notes for Facilitators'." National SEED Project. Accessed June 16, 2021. https://nationalseedproject.org/Key-SEED-Texts/white-privilege-unpacking-the-invisible-knapsack.

Schriefer, Paula. "What's the Difference between Multicultural, Intercultural, and Cross-Cultural Communication?" Spring Institute, March 11, 2020. https://springinstitute.org/whats-difference-multicultural-intercultural-cross-cultural-communication/.

Serwer, Adam. "The Fight Over the 1619 Project Is Not About the Facts." Medium. The Atlantic, December 26, 2019. https://medium.com/the-atlantic/the-fight-over-the-1619-project-is-not-about-the-facts-6bfacf987cb1.

Snyder, Michael. "19 Sad Facts About The Deindustrialization Of America." Business Insider. Business Insider, November 2, 2011. https://www.businessinsider.com/sad-facts-deindustrialization-america-2011-11#:~:text=But%20now%20we%20are%20witnessing,in%20the%20same%20time%20period.&text=Once%20upon%20a%20time%20America,rest%20of%20the%20world%20combined.

Sproul, R.C. "TULIP and Reformed Theology: Total Depravity." Ligonier Ministries, March 25, 2017. https://www.ligonier.org/blog/tulip-and-reformed-theology-total-depravity/.

Stafford, Tim. "How God Won When Politics Failed." ChristianityToday.com. Christianity Today, January 10, 2000. https://www.christianitytoday.com/ct/2000/january10/2.47.html.

Stafford, Tim. "The Abolitionists." Christian History | Learn the History of Christianity & the Church. Christian History, January 1, 1992. https://www.christianitytoday.com/history/issues/issue-33/abolitionists.html.

W., Stott John R. Through the Bible through the Year: Daily Reflections from Genesis to Revelation. Oxford: Monarch Books, 2014.

Storms, Sam. "The Goodness of God and Common Grace." The Gospel Coalition. Accessed June 17, 2021. https://www.thegospelcoalition.org/essay/goodness-god-common-grace/.

Thomas, Shari, and Tami Resch. "Two Basic Theological Frameworks: Contextualization and Theology." Essay by Tim Keller in Beyond Duct Tape: Holding the Heart Together in a Life of Ministry. Parakaleo, 2011.

Tisby, Jemar. How to Fight Racism: Courageous Christianity and the Journey toward Racial Justice. Grand Rapids, MI: Zondervan Reflective, 2021.

Tisby, Jemar. The Color of Compromise: the Truth about the American Church's Complicity in Racism. Chicago, IL: Zondervan, 2020.

Tyson, Timothy B. Blood Done Sign My Name: a True Story. New York: Broadway Books, 2013.

Wills, Matthew. "'How Prerequisite Cases Tried to Define Whiteness.'" JSTOR Daily. JSTOR.org, September 4, 2020. https://daily.jstor.org/how-prerequisite-cases-tried-to-define-whiteness/.

Yancey, George A. Beyond Racial Gridlock: Embracing Mutual Responsibility. Downers Grove, IL: InterVarsity Press, 2006.

Yancey, George. "Not White Fragility-Mutual Responsibility." The Gospel Coalition, July 27, 2020. https://www.thegospelcoalition.org/article/white-fragility-mutual-responsibility/.

Yancy, George. "Robin D.G. Kelley: The Tulsa Race Massacre Went Way Beyond 'Black Wall Street.'" Truthout, June 1, 2021. https://truthout.org/articles/robin-kelley-business-interests-fomented-tulsa-massacre-as-pretext-to-take-land/.

Yoshinaga, Kendra, and Bill Chappell. "Babies Of Color Are Now The Majority, Census Says." NPR. NPR, July 1, 2016. https://www.npr.org/sections/ed/2016/07/01/484325664/babies-of-color-are-now-the-majority-census-says .

ENDNOTES

Chapter 1
1 Christine D. Pohl, Living into Community: Cultivating Practices That Sustain Us (Grand Rapids, MI: Eerdmans, 2012), p. 2.

History Window 1
1 David French, "When Our Forefathers Fail," The French Press (The Dispatch, May 30, 2021), https://frenchpress.thedispatch.com/p/when-our-forefathers-fail.

Chapter 2
1 David P. Murray, The Happy Christian: Ten Ways to Be a Joyful Believer in a Gloomy World (Nashville, TN, TN: Nelson Books, 2015).p. 209.

History Window 2
2 Adam Hochschild, Bury the Chains: Prophets and Rebels in the Fight to Free an Empire's Slaves (Boston: Houghton Mifflin, 2006). p. 2.
3 "Slavery in Portugal," Wikipedia (Wikimedia Foundation, July 22, 2021), https://en.wikipedia.org/wiki/Slavery_in_Portugal.

History Window 3
4 "Guns Germs & Steel: Variables. Smallpox," PBS (Public Broadcasting Service), accessed August 3, 2021, https://www.pbs.org/gunsgermssteel/variables/smallpox.html#:~:text=Within%20just%20a%20few%20generations,the%20population%20of%20the%20Americas.
5 "Bartolomé De Las Casas," Wikipedia (Wikimedia Foundation, July 30, 2021), https://en.wikipedia.org/wiki/Bartolom%C3%A9_de_las_Casas.

Chapter 4
1 "Sunday Morning in America Still Segregated – and That's Ok With Worshippers," Lifeway Research, December 22, 2020, https://lifewayresearch.com/2015/01/15/sunday-morning-in-america-still-segregated-and-thats-ok-with-worshipers/.
2 Beck, John. Basic Bible Atlas (Grand Rapids, MI: Baker Book House, 2020). p. 127.

3 Ibid.

History Window 4
6 Baptist, Edward. p. xxiii-xxiv, xxv.
7 Matthew Desmond, "American Capitalism Is Brutal. You Can Trace That to the Plantation.," The New York Times (The New York Times, August 14, 2019), https://www.nytimes.com/interactive/2019/08/14/magazine/slavery-capitalism.html.
8 DiAngelo, Robin. White Fragility. Beacon Press: 2018. p. 5.

Chapter 5
1 Keller, Tim. "Two Basic Theological Frameworks: Contextualization and Theology." Essay in Beyond Duct Tape: Holding the Heart Together in a Life of Ministry by Thomas, Shari, and Tami Resch. Parakaleo, 2011.

Chapter 6
1 Leonard Pitts, "'I'm Not a Racist' Is Not a Good Defense for Racist Behavior," www.baltimoresun.com (The Baltimore Sun, June 15, 2020), https://www.baltimoresun.com/opinion/op-ed/bs-ed-op-0616-pitts-not-a-racist-20200615-uvgyfwnopvfbzd5xommn6i6r7y-story.html.
2 Sproul, R. C. (2017, March 25). TULIP and Reformed Theology: Total Depravity.
Ligonier Ministries. https://www.ligonier.org/blog/tulip-and-reformed-theology- total-depravity
3 Bob Burns, Tasha Chapman, and Donald Guthrie, Resilient Ministry: What Pastors Told Us About Surviving and Thriving (Downers Grove, IL: IVP Books, 2013). p. 147.
4 "Divided by Faith?" ChristianityToday.com (Christianity Today, October 2, 2000), https://www.christianitytoday.com/ct/2000/october2/1.34.html.

History Window 6
9 Jemar Tisby, The Color of Compromise: The Truth about the American Church's Complicity in Racism (Grand Rapids, MI: Zondervan, 2020). p. 209.

Chapter 7
1 Ince, Irwyn L. Jr. The Beautiful Community: Unity, Diversity, and the Church at Its Best (Downers Grove, IL: InterVarsity Press, 2020). p. 97-98.
2 Esau McCaulley, Reading While Black (Downers Grove, IL: InterVarsity Press, 2020), p. 116.
3 Ibid.

History Window 7
    10 Harris, John. The Last Slave Ship. New Haven: Yale University Press. p. 243-246.

Chapter 8
    1 McCaulley, Esau. Reading While Black. p. 112.
    2 Ince, Irwyn. The Beautiful Community. p. 93.

History Window 8
    11 Hochschield., Adam. Bury the Chains New York: Houghton Mifflin, 2005. p. 366.
    12 Harris, John. The Last Slave Ship. New Haven: Yale University Press. p. 243-246.
    13 "Genetic Impact of African Slave Trade Revealed in DNA Study," BBC News (BBC, July 24, 2020), https://www.bbc.com/news/world-africa-53527405.
    14 Tim Stafford, "The Abolitionists: Christian History Magazine," Christian History Institute, accessed March 10, 2021, https://christianhistoryinstitute.org/magazine/article/abolitionists.
    15 "John Brown," American Battlefield Trust, accessed August 4, 2021, https://www.battlefields.org/learn/biographies/john-brown?ms=googlegrant&gclid=CjwKCAjw9aiIBhA1EiwAJ_GTStz1ry6-rpU_eLdgcUmy26vBX80AIG2SNtG87mK-IAVoAvBkioUYEBoC0CMQAvD_BwE.

Chapter 9
    1 Murray, David. The Happy Christian.
    2 Thabiti Anyabwile, "Learning to Be the Moral Minority from a Moral Minority," The Gospel Coalition, February 4, 2013, https://www.thegospelcoalition.org/blogs/thabiti-anyabwile/learning-to-be-the-moral-minority-from-a-moral-minority.
    3 Stott John R W., Through the Bible through the Year: Daily Reflections from Genesis to Revelation (Oxford: Monarch Books, 2014).
    4 "In U.S., Decline of Christianity Continues at Rapid Pace," Pew Research Center's Religion & Public Life Project, June 9, 2020, https://www.pewforum.org/2019/10/17/in-u-s-decline-of- christianity-continues-at-rapid-pace/.

History Window 9
    16 "Carlisle Indian School Digital Resource Center," "Kill the Indian, and Save the Man." Capt. Richard H. Pratt on the Education of Native Americans | Carlisle Indian School Digital Resource Center, accessed June

10, 2021, http://carlisleindian.dickinson.edu/teach/kill-indian-and-save-man-capt-richard-h-pratt-education-native-americans.
17 "American Indian Boarding Schools Haunt Many" National Public Radio. May 12, 2008. https://www.npr.org/templates/story/story.php?storyId=16516865#:~:text=The%20federal%20government%20began%20sending,developed%20in%20an%20Indian%20prison.
18 "American Indian Boarding Schools." Wikipedia. https://en.wikipedia.org/wiki/American_Indian_boarding_schools. Accessed May 2021.
19 "History of Native Americans in the United States." Wikipedia. https://en.wikipedia.org/wiki/History_of_Native_Americans_in_the_United_States. Accessed May 2021.

Chapter 10

1 Michael O. Emerson and Christian Smith, Divided by Faith: Evangelical Religion and the Problem of Race in America (Oxford, NY: Oxford University Press, 2000). p. 170
2 Korie Little Edwards, "The Multiethnic Church Movement Hasn't Lived up to Its Promise," ChristianityToday.com (Christianity Today, February 16, 2021), https://www.christianitytoday.com/ct/2021/march/race-diversity-multiethnic-church-movement- promise.html.
3 "The King Philosophy - Nonviolence365®," The King Center, January 5, 2021, https://thekingcenter.org/about-tkc/the-king-philosophy/.
4 Batalova, Jeanne; Hanna, Mary; and Levesque, Christopher. "Frequently Requested Statistics on Immigration and Immigrants in the U.S." Migration Policy Institute. https://www.migrationpolicy.org/article/frequently-requested-statistics-immigrants-and- immigration-united-states-2020. Feb. 11.2021
5 Yoshinaga, Kendra. "Babies of Color are Now the Majority, Census Says." https://www.npr.org/sections/ed/2016/07/01/484325664/babies-of-color-are-now-the-majority- census-says . July 1, 2016.
6 "The Asian Population: 2010." The United States Census. Published March 2012. https://www.census.gov/prod/cen2010/briefs/c2010br-11.pdf.
7 "Chinese Immigration" https://www.pbs.org/opb/historydetectives/feature/chinese- immigration/
8 Frey, William H. "The U.S. Will Become Minority White in 2045, Census Projects." The Brookings Institute. https://www.brookings.edu/blog/the-avenue/2018/03/14/the-us-will-become-minority- white-in-2045-census-projects/. Sept. 10, 2018.
9 Passel, Jeffrey S. and Cohn, D'Vera. "U.S. Population Projections: 2005-2050." Pew Research Center. https://www.pewresearch.org/hispanic/

2008/02/11/us-population-projections-2005-2050/. Feb. 11, 2008.
10 Parker, Kim and Igielnik. "On the Cusp of Adulthood and Facing an Uncertain Future." Pew Research. https://www.pewresearch.org/social-trends/2020/05/14/on-the-cusp-of-adulthood-and- facing-an-uncertain-future-what-we-know-about-gen-z-so-far-2/. May 14, 2020
11 Ibid.
12 Ibid.
13 Edwards, Korie. "The Multiethnic Church Movement Hasn't Lived up to its Promise." Christianity Today. https://www.christianitytoday.com/ct/2021/march/race-diversity-multiethnic-church- movement-promise.html. Feb. 16, 2021.
14 Ibid.
15 Robertson, Campbell. A Quiet Exodus: Why Black Worshipers Are Leaving White Evangelical Churches https://www.nytimes.com/2018/03/09/us/blacks-evangelical-churches.html. March 9, 2018.
16 Kristin Du Mez, "#Leave Loud and the Evangelical Reckoning," Anxious Bench (Patheos, March 18, 2021), https://www.patheos.com/blogs/anxiousbench/2021/03/leaveloud-and-the-evangelical- reckoning/.

History Window 10

20 Matthew Wills, "How Prerequisite Cases Tried to Define Whiteness," JSTOR Daily (JSTOR.org, September 4, 2020), https://daily.jstor.org/how-prerequisite-cases-tried-to-define- whiteness/.
21   Gee, Buck and Peck, Denise. "Asian Americans Are the Least Likely Group in the U.S. to Be Promoted to Management" Harvard Business Review. https://hbr.org/2018/05/asian-americans-are-the-least-likely-group-in-the-u-s-to-be-promoted-to-management. May 31, 2018.

Chapter 11

1 "Slavery, United States," Slavery, United States - Places in History (Library of Congress), accessed June 9, 2021, https://www.loc.gov/rr/geogmap/placesinhistory/archive/2011/20110318_slavery.html.
  Randy Nabors, Insufficient: Pursuing Grace-Based Pastoral Competence (White Blackbird Books, 2020). p. 224.
2 Hill, Daniel. White Awake, p. 79.
3 "White Christians Have Become Even Less Motivated to Address Racial Injustice," Barna Group, accessed June 9, 2021, https://www.barna.com/research/american- christians-race-problem/.

History Window 11

22   U.S. Census Bureau, "Hispanic Heritage Month 2020," The United

States Census Bureau, September 22, 2020, https://www.census.gov/newsroom/facts-for-features/2020/hispanic-heritage-month.html.
23 Richard Edelman, "Our America: A Hispanic History of the United States," Edelman, accessed June 12,
2021, https://www.edelman.com/insights/our-america-hispanic-history-united-states.
24 History.com Editors. "Hispanic History Milestones: Timeline." History.com. A&E Television Networks, September 14, 2020. https://www.history.com/topics/hispanic-history/hispanic-latinx-milestones.
25 Edelman, Richard.
26 Marie Arana, "Perspective | A History of Anti-Hispanic Bigotry in the United States," The Washington Post (WP Company, August 9, 2019), https://www.washingtonpost.com/outlook/a-history-of-anti-hispanic-bigotry- in-the-united-states/2019/08/09/5ceaacba-b9f2-11e9-b3b4-2bb69e8c4e39_story.html.

Chapter 12
1 Edwards, Brad. "The Church of Individualism" Mere Orthodoxy. Sept. 2020. https://mereorthodoxy.com/the-church-of-individualism/.
2 Hamren, Kelly. "Social Justice, Critical Race Theory, Marxism, and Biblical Ethics." Christianity Today. July 3, 2020. https://www.christianitytoday.com/edstetzer/2020/june/reflections-from-christian- scholar-on-social-justice-critic.html.
3 Mathison, Keith. "All Truth is God's Truth—A Reformed Approach to Science and Scripture." Ligioner Ministries. May 11, 2012. https://www.ligonier.org/blog/all-truth-gods-truth-reformed-approach-science-and- scripture/.
4 Storms, Sam. "The Goodness of God and Common Grace." The Gospel Coalition.https://www.thegospelcoalition.org/essay/goodness-god-common-grace/. Accessed April 2021.

History Window 12
27 Arana, Marie. Ibid.
28 Arana, Marie.Ibid.
29 History.com, ibid.
30 Gerardo Marti and by: Mark T. Mulder, "More than a Fiesta -- Variety and Diversity among Latino Protestants in the U.S.," Faith and Leadership, Duke University, September 18, 2018. https://faithandleadership.com/gerardo-marti-and-mark-t-mulder-more-fiesta-variety-and- diversity-among-latino-protestants-us.
31 Daniel Cox and Robert P. Jones, "America's Changing Religious Identity," PRRI, accessed June 12, 2021, https://www.prri.org/research/

american-religious-landscape-christian-religiously- unaffiliated/.
32 Marti and Mulder, 2018.

Chapter 13

1 Oxford Essential Quotations. 5th edition. Oxford University Press, 2017. https://www.oxfordreference.com/view/10.1093/acref/9780191843730.001.0001/q-oro-ed5- 00000730.
2 Hill, Daniel. White Awake, p. 158.
3 Rah, S.-C. (2015). In prophetic lament: A call for justice in troubled times (pp. 64–65, 68.). IVP Books, an imprint of InterVarsity Press. 64-65, 68.
4 Edwards, Frank; Lee, Hedwig and Esposito, Michael. Risk of being killed by police use of force in the United States by age, race-ethnicity and sex. Proceedings of the National Academy of Sciences. https://www.pnas.org/content/116/34/16793. Aug. 20,2019.
5 Parker, K., Horowitz, J. M., & Anderson, M. (2020, December 17). Majorities Across Racial, Ethnic Groups Express Support for the Black Lives Matter Movement. Pew Research Center's Social & Demographic Trends Project. https://www.pewresearch.org/social-trends/2020/06/12/amid-protests-majorities- across-racial-and-ethnic-groups-express-support-for-the-black-lives-matter- movement/.
6 Alexander, Michelle. The New Jim Crow. The New Press, 2012. p. 98
7 "Mass Incarceration," American Civil Liberties Union, accessed August 3, 2021, https://www.aclu.org/issues/smart-justice/mass-incarceration.
8 Freeman, James. Wall Street Journal. July 23, 2020. https://www.wsj.com/articles/black-lives- matter-and-the-family-11595530123
9 Campbell, A. What is Black Lives Matter and what are the aims? BBC News. June 12, 2021. https://www.bbc.com/news/explainers-53337780.

History Window 13

2. Tisby, p. 8-87.

Chapter 14

1 Dana Rudolph, "White Privilege: Unpacking the Invisible Knapsack' and 'Some Notes for Facilitators'," National SEED Project, accessed June 16, 2021, https://nationalseedproject.org/Key-SEED-Texts/white-privilege-unpacking-the-invisible- knapsack.
2 Merriam-Webster. (n.d.). White Supremacy. Merriam-Webster. https://www.merriam- webster.com/dictionary/white%20supremacy.
3 Yancey, George A. Beyond Racial Gridlock: Embracing Mutual Responsibility. Downers Grove, IL: InterVarsity Press, 2006. P. 70.
4 Yancey, George, "Not White Fragility-Mutual Responsibility." The Gospel Coalition, July 27, 2020. https://www.thegospelcoalition.org/article/white-

fragility-mutual-responsibility/.
more power and thus have set up laws and policies that favored them.
5 Yancey, George, "Not White Fragility-Mutual Responsibility." The Gospel Coalition, July 27, 2020. https://www.thegospelcoalition.org/article/white-fragility-mutual- responsibility/.
6 John McWhorter, "The Dehumanizing Condescension of 'White Fragility'," The Atlantic (Atlantic Media Company, July 15, 2020), https://www.theatlantic.com/ideas/archive/2020/07/dehumanizing-condescension-white- fragility/614146/.
7 Yancey, 2006, p.
8 Yancey, 2006. P. 80.
9 Yancey, 2006, p. 87.
10 Yancey, 2020.

History Window 14
33 Tisby, ibid. p. 100.
34 "A Brief History of Jim Crow," Constitutional Rights Foundation, accessed June 11, 2021, https://www.crf-usa.org/black-history-month/a-brief-history-of-jim-crow.

Chapter 15
1 Dalyrample, Timothy. "Justice Too Long Delayed." Christianity Today, June 10, 2020. https://www.christianitytoday.com/ct/2020/june-web-only/justice-too-long-delayed.html
2 "White Christians Have Become Less Motivated to Address Injustice" Barna research. Sept. 15, 2020. https://www.barna.com/research/american-christians-race-problem/
3 "White Christians Have Become Even Less Motivated to Address Racial Injustice." Barna Research. https://www.barna.com/research/american-christians-race-problem/. Sept. 15, 2020. 4 (U.S. Dept. Of Education Office for Civil Rights)
4. "K-12 Disparity Facts and Statistics," UNCF (UNCF , March 20, 2020), https://uncf.org/pages/k-12-disparity-facts-and-stats.
5 Go Deeper—Where Race Lives." Race—The Power of an Illusion. PBS.org https://www.pbs.org/race/000_About/002_06-godeeper.htm.
6 Ortiz V;Telles E; "Racial Identity and Racial Treatment of Mexican Americans," Race and social problems (U.S. National Library of Medicine), accessed June 16, 2021.
7"Racial and Ethnic Disparities Continue in Pregnancy-Related Deaths," Centers for Disease Control and Prevention (Centers for Disease Control and Prevention, September 6, 2019), https://www.cdc.gov/media/releases/2019/p0905-racial-ethnic-disparities-pregnancy-deaths.html.

History Window 15
  35 Katznelson, Ira. When Affirmative Action Was White. Norton: 2006. p. 23.

Chapter 16
  1 Butterfield, Rosaria. Christianity Today, https://www.christianitytoday.com/ct/2018/april- web-only/rosaria-butterfield-gospel-comes-house-key.html
  2 Pohl, Christine. Making Room. Grand Rapids: Eerdmans, 1999. p. 75.
  3 Newbigin, Lesslie, Foolishness to the Greeks, p. 146, as quoted in Resilient Ministry (Burns, Chapman, and Guthrie).

History Window 16
  36 Katznelson, Ira. When Affirmative Action was White: An Untold History of Racial Inequality in Twentieth-century America. Nelson: 2005. p. 114.
  37   Robert Rowthorn, Robert and Ramaswamy, Ramana. "Deindustrialization-It's Causes and Implications." International Monetary Fund. Sept. 1997. https://www.imf.org/EXTERNAL/PUBS/FT/ISSUES10/INDEX.HTM.
  38   Snyder, Michael."The Sad Facts About the Deindustrialization of America." Business Insider. Nov. 2, 2011.https://www.businessinsider.com/sad-facts-deindustrialization-america-2011-11#:~:text=But%20now%20we%20are%20witnessing,in%20the%20same%20time%20period.&text=Once%20upon%20a%20time%20America,rest%20of%20the%20world%20combined.
  39 "Criminal Justice Facts." The Sentencing Project.

Chapter 17
  1 Kraus, Michael and Richeson, Jennifer. "The Wealth Gap Facing Black Americans is Vast-And Vastly Underestimated." https://insights.som.yale.edu/insights/the-wealth-gap-facing-black- americans-is-vast-and-vastly-underestimated. July 15, 2020
  2 Ibid.

History Window 17
  40 Tisby, p. 132.
  41 Tyson, Blood Done Sign My Name. p. 320

Chapter 18
  1 Ince, p. 114

2 Nathan Cartagena, "What Christians Get Wrong About Critical Race Theory – Part I," Faithfully Magazine, December 29, 2020, https://faithfullymagazine.com/critical-race- theory-christians/.
3 Anthony Bradley, "Critical Race Theory Isn't a Threat for Presbyterians," Mere Orthodoxy, February 3, 2021, https://mereorthodoxy.com/critical-race-theory-presbyterian-church-in-america/.
4 Joe Carter, "What Christians Should Know About Intersectionality," The Gospel Coalition, March 29, 2017, https://www.thegospelcoalition.org/article/what-christians-should-know- about-intersectionality/.
5 Ibid.
6 Anthony Bradley, "Critical Race Theory Isn't a Threat for Presbyterians," Mere Orthodoxy, February 3, 2021, https://mereorthodoxy.com/critical-race-theory-presbyterian-church-in-america/.
7 Ibid.
8 Kelly Hamren, Ed Stetzer, and Sadiri Joy Tira, "Social Justice, Critical Race Theory, Marxism, and Biblical Ethics," The Exchange | A Blog by Ed Stetzer, accessed June 17, 2021, https://www.christianitytoday.com/edstetzer/2020/june/reflections-from-christian- scholar-on-social-justice-critic.html.
9 Ibid.
10 Timothy Keller, "A Biblical Critique of Secular Justice and Critical Theory," Life in the Gospel, September 30, 2020, https://quarterly.gospelinlife.com/a-biblical-critique-of- secular-justice-and-critical-theory/.
11 Ibid.
12 Ibid.
13 Ibid.
14 Ibid.

History Window 18
    42 Tyson, p. 319-320
    43 Tyson, ibid. p. 306.
    44 Georgetown University, "Slavery, Memory and Reconciliation." http://slavery.georgetown.edu/. Accessed Dec. 2019.

Study 2
    David W. Augsburger, Caring Enough to Hear and Be Heard (Ventura, CA: Regal Books, 1983).

Study 4
    1 Basic Bible Atlas, p. 128.
    2 Race - The Power of an Illusion. Go Deeper." PBS. Public Broadcasting

Service. Accessed June 17, 2021. https://www.pbs.org/race/000_About/002_06-godeeper.htm.

Study 7
1 McCaulley, Esau. Reading While Black: African American Biblical Interpretation as an Exercise in Hope. Intervarsity Press, 2020. p. 116.

Study 9
1 Ince, p. 58-59

Study 10
1 McCaulley, Esau. Reading While Black: African American Biblical Interpretation as an Exercise in Hope. p. 114.
2 Paula Schriefer, "What's the Difference between Multicultural, Intercultural, and Cross- Cultural Communication?," Spring Institute, March 11, 2020, https://springinstitute.org/whats-difference-multicultural-intercultural-cross-cultural- communication/.

Study 12
1 Ellis, 2018
2 ibid.

Study 13
1 Where Do We Go from Here? Barna Research, 2019. p. 26

Study 14
1. Randy Nabors, Insufficient: Pursuing Grace-Based Pastoral Competence (White Blackbird Books, 2020). p. 226-27.
   Ibid.

Study 15
1 McCaulley, Reading While Black. Downers Grove: Intervarsity Press. 2020.p. 94

Study 17
(Hope for New York)

Study 18
6 Dalyrample, Timothy. "Justice Too Long Delayed." Christianitytoday.com. June, 2020. https://www.christianitytoday.com/ct/2020/june-web-only/justice-too-long-delayed.html

Made in the USA
Monee, IL
18 May 2022